OLDEST
LOS ANGELES

MIMI SLAWOFF

REEDY PRESS

Library of Congress Control Number: 2021952431

ISBN: 9781681063744

Cover Design: Jill Halpin

Book Design: Linda Eckels

All photos are by Mimi Slawoff unless otherwise stated.

Printed in the United States of America

22 23 24 25 26   5 4 3 2 1

Table of Contents

Greater Los Angeles Area

Hollywood

West L.A.

South Bay

San Gabriel Valley/Crescenta Valley

San Fernando Valley

Santa Clarita Valley

Santa Catalina Island

ACKNOWLEDGMENTS

Special thanks to my Bulgarian parents, Slatka and Stoitcho Slawoff, who immigrated to Los Angeles, where they raised my sister Doris and me to embrace our heritage and other cultures around us while assimilating.

I enjoyed writing about my hometown and appreciate the support I got from everyone who was involved in some way. Thank you to my husband, Bruce Mendelson, our kids Christina, Michael, and Megan, and my friends (especially my neighbor Donna Shiroma) who traveled across L.A. with me as I researched historic places and took photos for *Oldest Los Angeles*. I met a lot of friendly and helpful people (and made some new friends) along the way, confirming what I know is true—that L.A. is a welcoming city steeped in history that in some way connects all of us who live here.

I also want to express my gratitude to the Reedy Press team, a great group of people who were always available for questions and guidance.

In addition, the following people provided tips and useful information for this book:

Mike Lawler, local historian and author

Emily Wooten, El Pueblo de Los Angeles Historical Monument, History Division/ Special Events & Filming Division

Betty L. Uyeda, MLS, Collections Manager, Seaver Center for Western History Research, Natural History Museum of Los Angeles County.

INTRODUCTION

Los Angeles—which means The Angels in Spanish—is a sprawling city in Southern California that means different things to different people. For me, Los Angeles, nicknamed City of Angels and more commonly called L.A., is about the people—then and now.

From its birth in 1781, when an ethnically diverse group of 44 settlers arrived in what is now downtown, Los Angeles has evolved into 88 incorporated cities, home to over 10 million people from around the world.

Located within the 4,084-square-mile Los Angeles County, these cities reflect the ethnic diversity of Los Angeles. Immigrants like my Bulgarian parents and their friends settled in neighborhoods, forming their own communities, starting businesses and sharing their traditions while assimilating to their new surroundings.

Oldest Los Angeles explores these cities and neighborhoods, some big, some small, and shares stories from the people who helped shape L.A., creating a delightful melting pot. As families established restaurants, bakeries, markets, flower shops, theaters, and a multitude of other businesses, L.A. developed into a diverse city with many layers that reveal the faces and cultures of L.A., from the past to the present.

As a first-generation Bulgarian American and native Angeleno, I enjoy digging into L.A.'s past and exploring L.A. County with my three kids and visiting family and friends. There's always something to please everyone, and I share some of these in *Oldest Los Angeles*.

Beaches? L.A. has 75 miles of sand and surf from Long Beach to Malibu, with historic lighthouses, piers, parks, and hidden canals. L.A. also has an abundance of outdoor spaces, with decades-old botanical gardens and even a 250-year-old grapevine still producing grapes.

The arts and culture scene boasts world-class theaters and museums, and the world's largest active excavation site where fossils from the Ice Age are still being discovered. And, of course, L.A. is known for glitz, glamour, and grit, but authentic Old Hollywood is best experienced in old-timey restaurants, venues, bars, and historic homes.

Oldest Los Angeles also visits the site of California's first gold discovery in Newhall, a northern L.A. County town where there's also a hidden ghost town, and a park that's home to roaming bison.

What's amazing is that despite the fact I've lived in L.A. my entire life, I'm still discovering places like the oldest bowling alley, oldest dive bar, and a pharmacy with an old-fashioned soda fountain. So, while *Oldest Los Angeles* takes a journey to L.A.'s past and features over 84 oldest places, there are hundreds more to discover.

DOWNTOWN
LOS ANGELES

OLDEST LOS ANGELES DISTRICT

EL PUEBLO DE LOS ANGELES HISTORICAL MONUMENT

125 Paseo Pueblo de La Plaza

Situated in Downtown L.A., El Pueblo de Los Angeles Historical Monument marks the birthplace of the city. While the Gabrieleno-Tongva Indian Tribe first inhabited the L.A. basin, it was in September 1781 that 44 settlers of Native American, African, and European heritage established a farming community. As new settlers arrived, the humble pueblo evolved into a thriving community and L.A.'s incorporation as a city in 1850.

This oldest section of the city—a designated state historic park and a department of the City of Los Angeles since 1953—reflects the heritage of the many ethnic groups (Native American, Spanish,

The Pico House is part of El Pueblo de Los Angeles Historical Monument.

Mexican, Anglo, African American, Chinese, Italian and French) that contributed to L.A.'s early history.

El Pueblo traces the steps and stories of these early settlers. The district consists of 27 historic buildings: 11 are restored and open as businesses and free museums—Plaza Firehouse, Chinese American Museum, the América Tropical Interpretive Center, the Sepulveda House Museum, the Italian American Museum of Los Angeles, Avila Adobe, and the Museum of Social Justice. La Plaza de Cultura y Artes showcases performances and exhibits about Mexican and Mexican American history.

The hub is the 1820s plaza and Olvera Street Marketplace (opened in 1930). Both host popular events and festivals. The best way to explore El Pueblo is on free, guided or self-guided walking tours. Put on your walking shoes and step back into 19th- and 20th-century Los Angeles.

A good place to start is at the Plaza Firehouse, built in 1884 to house firefighting crews and their equipment. The neighboring Pico House, constructed between 1869-1870, was L.A.'s first three-story building and luxury hotel. Built by Pío Pico, the last governor of California under Mexican rule, the hotel had 80 bedrooms, 21 parlors, and bathrooms/water closets on each floor.

Debuting in1870 was the Merced Theatre, the first building dedicated to the theatre arts. The 1890 Garnier Building is the last surviving structure from the city's original Chinatown, and now houses the Chinese American Museum.

Nearby, La Iglesia de Nuestra Señora la Reina de Los Ángeles (Our Lady Queen of Angels Catholic Church) is an active parish built between 1818 and 1822.

Across the street, the América Tropical Interpretive Center showcases a once-controversial mural. The center is located inside the 1887 Sepulveda House, which represents the architectural and social transformation of Los Angeles from its early Mexican traditions to a blending of Mexican and Anglo culture.

Next door, there's a preserved Italian Hall—which was built as a gathering place for the Italian community in 1908—inside the Italian American Museum of Los Angeles.

The Pelanconi House was built between 1855-57 by Italian vintner Giuseppi Covaccichi and converted to the Casa La Golondrina restaurant in 1924. A tour highlight is the well-preserved 1818 Avila Adobe, situated on Olvera Street—a great place for an authentic Mexican meal!

Across the street, Los Angeles Union Station is a major transit hub that added to the pueblo area's reinvigoration. Built in a Mission Moderne style in 1939, the station features art deco chandeliers, inlaid marble floors, hand-painted mission tiles, shaded patios, palm trees, and a clock tower. 800 N Alameda St.

Los Angeles Union Station is the main railway station in Los Angeles.

OLDEST STANDING HOUSE

AVILA ADOBE

E-10 Olvera St.

L ocated in the heart of Olvera Street in El Pueblo de Los Angeles Historical Monument, the Avila Adobe was built in 1818 by Francisco José Avila. He was alcalde (mayor) of Los Angeles in 1810. The sturdy house, which reflects the lifestyle of California in the 1840s, was made of adobe brick (material consisting of clay, water, and other organic materials) and packed dirt for floors.

The Avila family traded cowhides and tallow from around the world to furnish their home. Avila's wife died in 1822, leaving him with three children. He remarried, and after his death in 1832, his second wife lived in the adobe.

In January 1847, during the Mexican-American War, Commodore Stockton and his troops found the house vacant and set up headquarters. In the years that

The Avila Adobe is an 1818 restored home in El Pueblo de Los Angeles Historical Monument.

The Avila Adobe's rooms are furnished circa late 1840s. Most are reproductions, but some are original.

followed, the Avila Adobe was rented to families and eventually became a boarding house. By 1928 the city condemned the adobe for unsanitary conditions and defective construction.

With the help of influential friends, a local woman named Christine Sterling restored the house, which was open for tours until it was weakened by the 1971 Sylmar earthquake. After a complete restoration, the Avila Adobe opened to the public as a museum. The rooms—a family room, kitchen, office, master bedroom, parlor, and children's room—are furnished circa late 1840s. While most furnishings are reproductions, some are original, including a black lacquer sewing box/table sometimes on display.

Listed on the National Register of Historic Places, the adobe is also designated as California State Landmark No. 145.

The grapes growing in the adobe's courtyard are believed to be from the 250-year-old grapevines at the San Gabriel Mission.

Oldest Plaza
Los Angeles Plaza
125 Paseo De La Plaza

L os Angeles Plaza is the hub of the 44-acre El Pueblo de Los Angeles Historical Monument, which marks the birthplace of the city and is home to numerous historic buildings. When then Governor Felipe de Neve founded the Pueblo de Los Angeles, he wanted a central plaza for the newly developing town.

Built in the 1820s as a monument to L.A.'s original settlers and four accompanying soldiers, the Plaza also served as a commercial center and gathering place for the growing community. A plaque listing the names of the settlers and additional plaques dedicated to the individual 11 families are in the ground encircling the Plaza's gazebo.

The original square plaza was renovated

The Plaza is the hub for various community events at El Pueblo de Los Angeles Historical Monument.

to a circular form and landscaped in the 1870s. The Plaza is home to two statues of historical significance: King Carlos III of Spain (the monarch who ordered the founding of the pueblo), and Spanish Governor Felipe de Neve, who selected the Pueblo's location and mapped out the town.

Cinco de Mayo is among the many celebrations that take place at the Plaza in El Pueblo de Los Angeles Historical Monument.

Originally, there was a third statue, that of Father Junipero Serra, founder of the Alta California missions. But his statue was among the many toppled in 2020 due to Serra's enslaving, arresting, and trying to change the cultural beliefs of Native Americans.

The Plaza continues to be the site for many festivals and community events, such as the popular Cinco de Mayo celebration.

The Placita de Dolores Bell replica in the Plaza represents Mexican independence from Spain in the early 1800s. The adjoining Los Angeles Plaza Park was developed after the 1930s.

OLDEST CHURCH IN THE CITY OF LOS ANGELES
LA IGLESIA DE NUESTRA SEÑORA LA REINA DE LOS ÁNGELES
535 N Main St.

L a Iglesia de Nuestra Señora la Reina de los Ángeles, also known as Our Lady Queen of Angels Catholic Church and informally as La Placita, is an active parish in El Pueblo de Los Angeles Historical Monument. It's the only building at El Pueblo that is still used for its original purpose, and serves as an active parish of the Roman Catholic Archdiocese of Los Angeles.

Sunday Masses, weddings, baptisms, First Communions, quinceañeras, and other special events take place at the church, which underwent several transformations since its beginning.

In 1784, construction began on the Roman Catholic Church, Nuestra Señora Reina de los Ángeles Asistencia (La Iglesia de Nuestra Senora de Los Angeles). It was the only Catholic church for the Pueblo at the time.

La Iglesia de Nuestra Senora la Reina de Los Angeles has been an active parish in Downtown L.A. since 1822.

Sunday masses, weddings, baptisms, and many other special events take place at an active parish La Iglesia de Nuestra Senora la Reina de Los Angeles.

Several years later, in 1814, Franciscan Fray Luis Gil y Taboada placed the cornerstone for the new church in the adobe ruins of the La Iglesia de Nuestra Senora de Los Angeles. On December 8, 1822, dedication ceremonies were held for the finished church sanctuary. Materials from the original church were used to build a replacement structure in 1861, La Iglesia de Nuestra Senora de Los Angeles. Later, the church's name was enhanced with the word Reina, or "Queen." It has been modified since the 1960s to withstand earthquakes. A mural of the Madonna and child, enthroned with angels, and framed pictures of saints are some of the artistic features of the church.

A California Historical Landmark, the church was among the first three landmarks in Los Angeles to gain Historic-Cultural Monument status in 1962.

La Placita began as a 1,400-square-foot chapel, located around the back of the church and now used primarily for baptisms and smaller services.

Oldest Surviving Brick House

The Pelanconi House

17 Olvera St.

Sitting in the middle of historic Olvera Street, the Pelanconi House was a winery that produced wine from locally grown grapes, possibly even across the street at the Avila Adobe. Grapevines still grow at the adobe.

The house was built by Italian vintner Giuseppi Covaccichi, a native of Gordona, Lombardia, between 1855-57. The house had living quarters on the second floor and a wine cellar below. The stone fireplace was used to make sherry. Cavacci and his partner, Giuseppe Gazzo, also operated a winery across the street.

The Pelanconi House changed hands four times until 1871, when it was purchased by winemaker Antonio Pelanconi.

The Pelanconi House started as a winery and was later converted to the Casa La Golondrina Mexican Cafe.

He continued operation of the winery until 1877, when he turned over the winery operation to his partner, Giacomo Tononi. Pelanconi lived in the house with his wife and children until his death in 1879.

His widow, Isabel, wed Tononi in 1881. Isabel and Lorenzo Pelanconi (her son with Antonio) built the Pelanconi Warehouse for wine storage in 1910.

In 1924, Señora Consuelo Castillo de Bonzo converted the Pelanconi House into a restaurant. She removed the rear wall of the warehouse and the Pelanconi House to make one large room for her restaurant, Casa La Golondrina, which opened its doors on April 30, 1930 for the opening-night party of Olvera Street.

Los Angeles had become the largest wine-producing area in the state by 1869, and Olvera Street originally was known as Wine Street, due to the many Plaza-area wineries. Italian vintners owned many of these facilities.

OLDEST SURVIVING THEATER BUILDING
MERCED THEATRE
420 N Main St.

T he Merced Theatre's opening on January 30, 1871 placed it at the heart of the performing arts scene in Los Angeles. The second-story, 400-seat theater opened with a performance of *Fanchon the Little Cricket*. Ticket prices at the opening ranged from 50 cents in the balcony to $1 for main-floor seats.

It was the first building in Los Angeles constructed for the theater arts and is the oldest surviving theater building. Designed by Ezra F. Kysor, the Merced Theatre was built in 1870 for businessman William Abbot, who named it after his wife, Maria Merced Gloria. The Merced Theatre, which became known for its satirical presentations, also

The Merced Theatre represents the history of the LGBTQ community around the turn of the 20th century.

showcased fashionable burlesque and minstrel performances and professional acting ensembles.

But the theater's success didn't last long. Steep competition with neighboring theaters and a local outbreak of smallpox led to a dramatic decline in ticket sales after only five years. Although the Merced Theatre closed as a performing arts space in 1877, it continued serving as an informal entertainment venue.

The building's proprietors provided rental quarters to gay men, beginning in 1897. At the turn of the 20th century, the theater began hosting masked balls where LGBTQ individuals could dress in the clothing they chose, regardless of gender, and hide their identities behind masks while they socialized with others. The fear of persecution and social stigma was removed at these events, which led to drag balls in later decades and helped to secure cross-gender costuming as a valid social subculture and a distinctive expression of art.

The Merced Theatre is one of a few locations left in Los Angeles that represents the history of the LGBTQ community during the late 19th and early 20th centuries.

Improvements both inside and out at the Merced Theatre were completed during the 1960s and 1980s. Now used as a warehouse, the building was unoccupied between 1985 and 2014.

Oldest Firehouse
Plaza Firehouse
501 N Los Angeles St.

One of seven free museums in El Pueblo de Los Angeles Historical Monument, the Plaza Firehouse contains firefighting equipment from the late 19th and early 20th centuries. These include helmets, photos, and firefighting equipment.

In the middle of the 19th century, the City of L.A. didn't have a fire department, fire extinguishing equipment, or fire stations, because homes were made of adobe and fires were rare at that time. And if there was a fire, neighbors would extinguish it by forming a bucket brigade, using whatever available water they had.

In 1869, citizens formed a volunteer fire department, prompting the city to establish a Council Committee of Fire and Water. The council contracted with the water company to install hydrants to supply water as needed. Two years later, a fire department was created, followed by the purchase of a steam fire engine and hose cart.

George P. McCain was the first engineer and paid employee, with a salary of $100 a month.

The Plaza Firehouse museum is filled with firefighting equipment and memorabilia from the late 19th and 20th centuries.

In 1874, a new volunteer company was formed, and it acquired a hook and ladder truck and two horses to pull the engine. The firehouse changed companies and volunteers until 1884, when the new firehouse was built by the City of Los Angeles. A turntable in the floor made it unnecessary to back the horses in and out. The first occupants of the new Plaza Firehouse were called the Volunteer 38s (the number of men in Engine Company No. 1).

In 1885, the first paid fire department was established. On-duty firemen were stationed on the top floor, while horses stabled on the ground floor. A hayloft was built above the horse stalls. When the alarm sounded, the firefighters slid down the brass pole. Advances were made in 1892, when a chemical engine with two cylinders holding 50 gallons of water and bicarbonate of soda provided strong pressure for pumping water.

The firehouse's site was privately owned by Mrs. L. M. Bigelow until the lease expired in1897. The city's decision to build all future fire stations on municipally owned land ended the Plaza Firehouse's role as a fire station.

Over the next 60 years the firehouse was used as a saloon, cheap boarding house, a cigar store, seedy hotel, a Chinese vegetable market, and drugstore until the State of California purchased the facility in 1954.

In 1953, the State of California joined with the City and County of Los Angeles to create El Pueblo de Los Angeles State Historic Park, now known as El Pueblo de Los Angeles Historical Monument. The Plaza Firehouse was restored and converted into a museum, which opened in 1960.

OLDEST SURVIVING CHINESE STRUCTURE

GARNIER BUILDING

425 N Los Angeles St.

L ocated on the site of the original Chinatown in downtown L.A., the Garnier Building is part of the 44-acre El Pueblo de Los Angeles Historical Monument. In 1890, French settler and prominent businessman Philippe Garnier built the Garnier Building, which he leased to Chinese merchants and organizations.

The building was the hub of Chinese cultural life for several decades, serving as the unofficial "city hall" of the Los Angeles Chinese community. It's where the local Chinese would shop, send their kids to school, and attend temple, from the 1890s to the 1940s.

The building also served as a gathering place for various social events, including dances and theater productions.

The community followed Chinese tradition by

The Garnier Building, the hub of Chinese cultural life for many decades, now houses the Chinese American Museum. Photo courtesy of the Chinese American Museum

designating the building's upper floors—believed to be closer to heaven—for its temples, schools, and leading fraternal and social organizations. The ground floor and mezzanine levels were for commercial customers.

The role of the upper level institutions was to oversee and resolve any differences between individuals and organizations and to provide care for the elderly and those in need. In addition, they acted as liaison with American society. After the Chinese Massacre of 1871 and the Chinese Exclusion Act of 1882 that lasted until 1943, the local Chinese faced prejudice and discrimination.

In fact, beginning in 1933, the City of Los Angeles forced the Chinese community to move from its original location in order to build the Union Station Passenger Terminal and freeways systems. Residents were evicted and buildings were demolished—except for the Garnier Building, which is the last surviving structure of the original Chinatown.

Housed in the historic Garnier Building, the 7200-square-foot Chinese American Museum (CAM) opened on December 18, 2003. CAM is dedicated to researching, preserving, and sharing the experiences and contributions of Chinese Americans in the United States through quality exhibitions, programs, events, publications, and workshops.

Oldest Historic Landmark
Bradbury Building
304 S Broadway

Over 100 years after the stately Bradbury was built, it's a popular tourist attraction, even though the general public can only admire its first floor. While the public is allowed to enter, visitors are allowed only in the lobby and on the first set of stairs.

The Bradbury was built in 1893 for office space. That was the vision of mining and real estate millionaire Lewis Bradbury. He had asked famed local architect Sumner Hunt to design it, but hired one of Hunt's draftsmen, George Wyman, to complete the design instead.

While the exterior is dark brick, the building's light-filled Victorian atrium rises 50 feet with open-cage elevators, marble stairs and ornate iron railings. The five-story central court features glazed and unglazed yellow and pink

Although the Bradbury Building contains offices, its architecture attracts tourists, who are only allowed access to the lobby.

The Bradbury Building's lobby has open-cage elevators, marble stairs and ornate iron railings. Photo courtesy of Los Angeles Tourism & Convention Board

bricks, ornamental cast iron, tiling, Italian marble, Mexican tile, decorative terra-cotta, and polished wood. The crowning glory is the skylight that lets in natural light and shadows. At the time the building was completed, it featured the largest plate-glass windows in Los Angeles.

The building's elegant interior architecture has been used in several films, including *Blade Runner* (1982) and *Chinatown* (1974). The Bradbury Building was designated a National Historic Landmark in 1977 and is L.A.'s oldest official landmark building.

Tucked into a narrow space next to the Bradbury Building is the Biddy Mason Memorial Park, which pays tribute to a former slave who came to California and fought for her freedom (1856). She was a mother of three, a nurse, midwife, philanthropist and landowner in 19th-century L.A. Situated on her former homestead, an 80-foot wall depicts her life with words and pictures. 333 S Spring St.

Oldest Public Art Sculpture
Spanish-American War Memorial
Artist: Goddard, S. M.
532 S Olive St.

Thousands of people, including most of the members of the Seventh Regiment of the National Guard of California, attended the ceremony for the dedication of the Spanish-American War Memorial on Memorial Day in 1900 in what was then called Central Park (it was renamed Pershing Square in 1918.)

Completed and installed in 1900, the granite sculpture memorializes 21 Southern California volunteers who died while serving in the Seventh Regiment during the Spanish-American War. The sculpture depicts a soldier wearing a uniform, a hat, a canteen, and a cartridge belt, and holding his rifle at parade rest.

The story behind the memorial begins on May 6, 1898, when the Seventh Regiment of the National Guard of California left Los Angeles by train to fight for America in its war with Spain. A month earlier, the United States had

Located in L.A.'s historic Pershing Square, the Spanish-American War Memorial honors the 21 Southern California volunteers who died in the Spanish-American War.

declared war against Spain to show its support of the ongoing struggle by Cubans and Filipinos against Spanish rule, in addition to the mysterious explosion of the battleship USS *Maine* in Havana Harbor.

The war ended with the signing of the Treaty of Paris in 1898 by Spain and the US. The treaty established the independence of Cuba, and ceded Puerto Rico, Guam, and the Philippines to the US.

Meanwhile, Private George W. Swing of Company K, Seventh Regiment, United States Volunteers, wrote letters to the Los Angeles Chamber of Commerce and Los Angeles City Park Commissioners, requesting assistance for funding and the placement of a monument dedicated to the memory of the soldiers in his regiment who died while serving in the Spanish-American War.

Since the monument's installation in 1900, permanent and temporary public art has been placed in Pershing Square.

The monument was recognized by the Los Angeles Cultural Heritage Commission as Cultural-Heritage Monument No. 480 in 1990.

Pershing Square, situated on original pueblo land dating back to 1781, is a public park in downtown Los Angeles. In 1866 it was known as La Plaza Abaja (the Lower Plaza). In 1918, one week after WWI, the square was renamed Pershing Square in honor of General John Pershing. Over the years, several changes were made to the park, including the addition of an underground parking garage in 1951. Today, Pershing Square is home to public art that represents the city's history

OLDEST FUNICULAR RAILWAY
ANGELS FLIGHT

Top Station, California Plaza, 350 S Grand Ave.
Lower Station, 351 S Hill St.

The Angels Flight funicular (a cable railway built on an incline) opened on New Year's Eve in 1901 to transport people between what was then an affluent residential neighborhood on Bunker Hill and the offices and shops below for a penny a ride. More than 2,000 people showed up for opening day.

Built by Col. James Ward Eddy, a railroad man and an Illinois lawyer friend of Abraham Lincoln, Angel's Flight has two funicular cars, Olivet and Sinai, running in opposite directions on a shared cable. It runs for only one block (298 feet), linking California Plaza at the top to Grand Central Market at the bottom.

The one-way fare rose to a nickel in 1914 and stayed at that rate until the railway was put into storage in 1969 while Bunker Hill was redeveloped into a modern commercial center. The Community Redevelopment Agency and the Los Angeles County Metropolitan Transportation Authority restored the funicular, which debuted again in 1996.

Since then, it has been operated and maintained by the nonprofit Angels Flight™ Railway Foundation. A one-way trip is $1, and with a Metro TAP card the fare is just 50 cents.

In 2017, several new safety features were installed. Taller plexiglass endgates have been added on the trams, and upgrades

The Angels Flight funicular, which was built to carry passengers between a residential neighborhood and shops, is more of a fun experience than a necessity today.

have been made to the railway's communications and control equipment. Despite the improvements, Angel's Flight retains its cool, vintage look. While it's more of a fun experience than a necessity, it still saves a few walking steps for today's pedestrians.

Not surprisingly, Angels Flight has been in more than 100 movies and TV shows. In August 1962, Angels Flight was designated Los Angeles Historic-Cultural Monument #4, and added to the National Register of Historic Places in October 2000.

Built in 1989 in the historic neighborhood of Bunker Hill, the Bunker Hill Steps (also called Library Steps) feature a 60-foot-wide architectural double stairway flanking cascading river rock and a concrete "stream" flowing into a fountain with concrete seating. W 5th St. and Hope Pl.

1903
OLDEST CONFECTIONERY
FUGETSU-DO
315 E First St.

For four generations, the Kito family has been making mochi (Japanese rice cakes), manju (sweet, bean-filled rice cake), and other traditional Japanese pastries at Fugetsu-Do in Little Tokyo.

Brian Kito grew up in the family business. As a young boy he learned to make the mochi and manju sold in Fugetsu-Do, started in 1903 by his grandfather, Seiichi Kito, an immigrant from Gifu in central Japan.

The store is so popular that even during COVID-19, when the Kitos limited the number of people inside to three, there was a line outside waiting to enter. The store's display cases are filled with the colorful pastry with names like sudare (white bean paste inside the mochi with a dense bean jelly, yokan, on top), pink (a pink mochi with white bean paste filling), kusa (a yomogi herb mixed into the mochi), and ogura (whole red bean on the outside and mochi inside).

Over the years there have been some changes.

Little Tokyo's Fugetsu-Do is a popular place for traditional mochi and manju.

"Some products are made by machine, but most are made by hand or finished by hand. Our peanut butter and chocolate are done totally by machine," said Kito.

Life hasn't been easy for the Kitos. In 1941, during World War II, Brian's Japanese American grandfather and dad were forced to go to internment camps. They bought the store back upon their return in 1946. Brian Kito, a master manju confectioner, attributes the store's survival to the perseverance of the Japanese people.

Just like his dad and the generations before him, Kito's son Korey has learned the art of making mochi. The shop has a steady business but is especially busy during holidays, festivals, and special events.

Family members work together pulling all-nighters to fill orders for holidays (the week between Christmas and New Year's is especially busy), Girl's Day (3/3) and Boy's Day (5/5). Even today, cousins send their children to Kito to help during the New Year rush.

In 2003, Brian Kito received a letter from a member of the Chinese American Historical Society of New England in Boston, MA, stating that it was a Japanese American in Los Angeles and not a Chinese who created the fortune cookie. Since Seiichi Kito had produced a sweet cracker for the outside of the fortune cookie, it's believed he created the fortune cookie. "So, my siblings and I finally believed the stories that my father had talked about," said Kito. The family's fortune cookie molds are in the Smithsonian in Washington, DC.

OLDEST OPERATING BAR
GOLDEN GOPHER
417 W 8th St.

Walking into this downtown dive bar is like stepping back in time. The long, dimly lit bar with a pool table and cigarette smoke wafting in from the outdoor patio feels like it's in a different era.

Located in the heart of downtown L.A., the Golden Gopher was restored (actually rescued, according to owner Cedd Moses) and reopened in 2004. But it took a lot of work to restore the bar, said Moses, who saw its potential and wrote about the process in his book, *Pouring with Heart* (Lioncrest Publishing, 2021).

"I was attracted to the bar based on its amazing history as a watering hole for the likes of writer Charles Bukowski. And it being the oldest existing dive bar in Los Angeles," said Moses.

The Golden Gopher's 1905 dual liquor license means customers can buy drinks to go.

When he visited the bar in 2001, it looked nothing like the bar he remembered from a decade prior. Now it was a dump, operating as a front for drug dealing and prostitution. Besides the rich history (Theodore Roosevelt was said to have visited in 1905), there was little good about the Golden Gopher left.

The Golden Gopher is a laid-back, rock n' roll dive bar in Downtown L.A.

He restored the bar in 2002, turning it into a rock 'n' roll dive bar with many historic features still intact. Near the entrance is a liquor-to-go counter and a sign that reads, Liquor Here, Liquor to Go, referring to the bar's original 1905 dual liquor license that exempts it from abiding by certain present-day ordinances, such as prohibiting the sale or location of alcohol within a certain distance of the establishment's front door, or the prohibition of liquor-to-go. So that means customers can order drinks from the counter or buy a six-pack of beer from the old-timey bar.

It's a fun, laid-back place where customers can sit at the bar, find cozy seating in or outdoors, and play a game or two of Pac-Man while enjoying a beer or cocktail.

"The Golden Gopher crawled out of the depths of despair to become a runaway success. Today, the bar is busier than ever, and its bartending positions are some of the most coveted in the city. It's a landmark of burgeoning downtown Los Angeles and has been honored by our city's mayor for being a shining beacon of light within the community." Excerpt from Pouring with Heart.

Oldest Italian Hall
The Italian Hall
644 N Main St.

After Mexico gained its independence from Spain in 1821, many Italians began immigrating to Los Angeles. Sailor Giovanni Leandri was the first Italian settler, arriving in1827. The earliest Italian community was located at the Plaza, where Italians lived and worked among Mexican, French, Anglo, and Chinese communities in the area now known as El Pueblo de Los Angeles Historical Monument.

In 1908, the growing and prospering Italian community built a community center with the words "Italian Hall" emblazoned in gold lettering on its yellow brick façade. The spacious hall, which had a stage and wood floors, served as a cultural and social center for meetings, speakers, concerts, weddings, and cultural events such as vendemmia, or fall wine harvest. Most Saturdays there was dancing and live music by the Pete Pontrelli Orchestra. It was also where immigrants who didn't speak English could get assistance with legal documents and other business matters. Historical individuals, luminaries, and stars, including crusader Emma Goldman, were embraced at the Italian Hall.

As other meeting places opened, patronage at the Italian Hall decreased by the 1930s. The building was sold in 1953 to the State of California. As the Italian community's use of the hall ceased, it fell into disrepair. When it faced demolition, the Italian community created a group, later known as the Historic

The Italian American Museum houses the original Italian Hall that was built in 1908 as a gathering place for the growing Italian community.

Italian Hall Foundation, to restore the Italian Hall and preserve its original wood floors and stage. It also created the Italian American Museum of Los Angeles (IAMLA), located inside the historic Italian Hall in 2016.

Listed on the National Register of Historic Places, the Italian Hall is the earliest existing building from the Italian settlement of Los Angeles.

Located inside the historic Italian Hall is the 5,000-square-foot Italian American Museum of Los Angeles (IAMLA), operated by the City of Los Angeles and the Historic Italian Hall Foundation. The museum has seven permanent exhibits with documents, photos, and documentary-style videos, in addition to rotating exhibits, that depict the history of Italian American pioneers in L.A.

OLDEST FRENCH DIP SANDWICH SHOP
PHILIPPE THE ORIGINAL
1001 N Alameda St.

Just as they have for decades, customers wait patiently in line (often out the door) for a French Dipped Sandwich at Philippe's, then eat it family-style at long tables on sawdust-covered floors. It's a longtime L.A. tradition that satisfies a craving for a carved roasted meat sandwich on bread that's dipped one or multiple times (your choice!) in savory pan juices. The tasty invention apparently happened inadvertently.

Philippe The Original is popular for its French Dipped Sandwiches.

In 1908, Philippe Mathieu opened a restaurant that served roasted meats. But it wasn't until 1918 when he was making a sandwich that he accidentally dropped the sliced French roll into the roasting pan filled with juice. His customer—a police officer—said he would take the sandwich anyway. He liked it so much he returned the next day with some friends and asked for more dipped sandwiches. So goes the story.

Customers can choose to have their French Dipped Sandwiches dipped one or more times in au juice.

What's not known is whether the sandwich got its name from either Mathieu's French heritage, the French roll the sandwich was made on, or because the officer's name was French.

In 1927, Mathieu sold Philippe's to Harry, Dave, and Frank Martin for $5,000. To make way for the Hollywood-Santa Ana 101 Freeway, Philippe's was forced to move and relocated to its present-day location in 1951.

Philippe's menu has stayed simple, and meals are served on paper plates. The French Dipped Sandwich is made with either roast beef, roast pork, leg of lamb, turkey, pastrami, or ham served on a freshly baked French roll, which is dipped in the natural gravy of the roasts. Swiss, American, Monterey Jack, or blue cheese may be added. For side dishes, Philippe's offers coleslaw, house-made potato and macaroni salads, hard-boiled eggs in beet juice and spices, dill or sweet pickles, black olives, and hot yellow chili peppers.

Philippe's prepares about 40 gallons of its signature hot mustard twice weekly. It's best used sparingly, as it is truly very hot French mustard.

OLDEST OPERATING PUB
COLE'S PACIFIC ELECTRIC BUFFET
118 E 6th St.

Cole's has several cool things going for it, starting with its historic location on the ground floor of the 10-story Pacific Electric Building, which was L.A.'s tallest skyscraper in the 1900s. It was also the main train station for the Pacific Electric Railway.

Founded by Henry Cole in 1908, Cole's is a restaurant and saloon also known for French dip sandwiches, which it takes credit for creating (and making in the same location since it opened) when a customer with sore gums asked for his roast beef sandwich to be dipped in juice to soften the crunchy roll.

With its location near L.A.'s financial center, Cole's was popular with businesspeople, prompting the owners to open a free check-cashing service—the city's first—in a cage at the back of the restaurant. Cole's outdoor sign still displays the word "payroll," but the "checks cashed" wording was removed years ago. According to the current owner, Cedd Moses, during Prohibition the chef would send out coffee cups full of illegal whiskey instead of coffee.

Moses bought and restored the place in 2007 and managed to reopen it in time for the public house's 100th anniversary. "In the old kitchen (which was in really bad shape), we built a now-famous bar called the Varnish, named after the most exclusive railcar on the Pacific Electric streetcars 100 years

Cole's is a hip, restored restaurant/bar that retains many original elements and serves sandwiches and classic cocktails.

ago," said Moses. They partnered with Sasha Petraske and Eric Alperin on the Varnish, which won best American Cocktail bar at the National Spirit Awards in 2016.

Varnish, located at the back of Cole's, opens at 7 p.m., but the pub opens earlier. The renovation added new elements—like a pool table—but the restaurant retains many of the original elements, such as the dark red wallpaper, Tiffany glass lampshades over the mahogany bar, penny-tiled floor, and a vintage clock.

Cole's occupies the ground level of the historic Pacific Electric Building, which opened on January 15, 1905. The Pacific Electric Building was the main train station, as well as the company's headquarters. The Main Street Station served passengers boarding trains for the south and east of Southern California. Today the building has loft apartments.

──────────────────────────────────1911

OLDEST REMAINING
ORPHEUM THEATRE
PALACE THEATRE
630 S Broadway

L ocated in the heart of the historic theater district, the Palace
Theatre opened on June 25, 1911 as the third home of the
Orpheum vaudeville circuit in Los Angeles. Originally known
as the "Orpheum," it's the oldest remaining Orpheum theatre in
the country.

In its prime, the Palace featured many famous performers,
including Al Jolson, the Marx Brothers, W. C. Fields, Will Rogers,
Harry Houdini, Will Rogers, Fred Astaire, and Rita Hayworth.

Designed by architect G. Albert Lansburgh (one of the principal
theater architects in the west between 1909 and 1930), the theater
is loosely styled after a Florentine, early Renaissance palazzo.

While the theater's exterior features
Italian influences, the interior decoration
is French, with garland-draped columns
and a color scheme of pale pastels. In its
prime, the luxurious theater had almost
2,000 seats on three levels, and no seats
were farther than 80 feet from the stage.

In the 1930s, the original box seats
were removed. In addition, the walls were

*The Palace Theatre features
panels depicting the four
muses of vaudeville—Song,
Dance, Music, and Drama.*

In its heyday, the Palace Theatre featured Al Jolson, the Marx Brothers, Fred Astaire, and many other famous performers. Photo courtesy of Los Angeles Tourism & Convention Board

plastered and painted over with murals by Candelario Rivas. The theater now seats about 1,000 people.

With the theater world growing, the Palace underwent changes over the years. It was renamed Broadway Palace in 1926, and featured musical comedy and variety, and became the News Palace in 1939 when it began showing newsreels and documentaries. By 1947, the theater once again became the Palace and reopened with the premiere engagement of *The Best Years of Our Lives*.

In 2011, the Palace Theatre celebrated its 100th birthday, following a $1 million renovation to restore the venue for concerts, film screenings, and special events.

Currently, the Palace is one of four theaters owned by the Broadway Theatre Group, which manages, restores, and preserves historic theaters. The Palace Theatre is listed on the National Register of Historic Places.

Downtown L.A.'s historic Broadway Theatre District spans six blocks along South Broadway and includes 12 movie theaters built between 1910 and 1931. Among them: The Orpheum Theatre, (842 S Broadway), which opened on February 15, 1926. The restored theater continues to host live music and is frequently used as a film location. The Broadway Theatre District was added to the National Register of Historic Places in May 1979, the first and largest historic theater district listed on the register.

OLDEST WINERY
SAN ANTONIO WINERY
737 Lamar St.

Italian immigrant Santo Cambianica's American dream came true when he founded the San Antonio Winery in 1917 in Los Angeles, then a prime grape-growing and winemaking region. Dedicating the winery to his patron saint, St. Anthony, he established a close-knit family business, now in its fourth generation.

From the beginning, family members worked together as a team to grow their business, which survived Prohibition by becoming the number one provider of altar wines for Catholic churches—a service it still provides.

When Stefano Riboli and his wife, Maddalena Satragni, inherited the winery in the 1950s, they looked for ways to expand. In 1970, matriarch Maddalena, who enjoyed cooking, opened Maddalena Restaurant, where century-old redwood casks line the walls. Located inside the winery, the restaurant's specialty is Maddalena's homemade lasagna, which pairs nicely with a cabernet sauvignon.

Stefano Riboli and wife Maddalena Satragni inherited San Antonio Winery in the 1950s. Photo courtesy of San Antonio Winery

San Antonio Winery is a family owned and operated winery and restaurant in Downtown L.A. Photo courtesy of San Antonio Winery

With the help of their children, the Ribolis purchased vineyard properties in Monterey County in the 1970s, Napa Valley in the 1980s, and later Paso Robles. The family continues to make and ferment white wines on-site, and bottle the red and white wines in L.A.

With each generation, family members pitch in at young ages, eventually finding their niche. Dante, a fourth-generation family member, has fond memories of working alongside his grandparents. Now the family's marketing director, he was just 10 or 11 when he started working at the restaurant cleaning bathrooms, busing tables, and washing dishes before being promoted to tasting room stock boy and host.

"Based off my first paycheck, that was only 10 years ago. So, I was definitely working for free for many, many years, as most of my family members did," he said. San Antonio Winery still sits on its original location on Lamar Street, the last vestige of the rich winemaking tradition of Greater Los Angeles.

San Antonio Winery tours take visitors through the winery gift shop, tasting room, fermentation tanks, bottling line, and historic rooms. Tastings are from a collection of wines from the family's estate vineyards in Napa Valley, Monterey County and Paso Robles.

1917

Oldest Public Market
Grand Central Market
317 S Broadway

The mouthwatering aromas of slow-cooked pork, chow mein, fried chicken, BBQ and other ethnic dishes pleasantly mingle in the 30,000-square-foot, open-air market, home to about 40 food stalls.

The bustling food court reflects the microcosm of the immigrant communities that shape L.A. Legacy vendors like China Cafe and Roast To Go have been tenants for over half a century. In addition, many new vendors have moved in to offer additional food and drink options.

When the market debuted in October 1917, it was billed as the Wonder Market. An early promotional booklet for the market boasted of 250-foot display cases, featuring everything from fish, oysters, and meat to the finest produce from farmers across the Southland.

The market replaced the Ville de Paris Store that occupied the first floor of the Beaux Arts-style Homer

Grand Central Market in the early days. Photo courtesy of GCS Equity LLC

Downtown L.A.'s Grand Central Market has about 40 food stalls offering a wide range of ethnic dishes.

Laughlin Building, the region's first steel-reinforced, fireproof structure. The market initially catered to affluent residents who lived in Bunker Hill mansions and would ride the Angels Flight funicular to shop at the market and return with their purchases.

After World War II, the expansion of freeways led the wealthy away from Downtown L.A. to new suburbs. The Bunker Hill mansions were eventually converted to low-income housing, before being demolished and replaced by skyscrapers.

Through all the changes, the market stayed open, changing its products and prices to meet the needs of the shifting local community. Today, the market is a gathering place for locals, and a popular tourist attraction.

In addition to prepared foods to enjoy on the spot, there's a butcher shop that sells organic meat, a produce stand, a Latin grocery store, a craft brewery, and many other vendors.

Grand Central Market hosts a variety of events, including the weekly Grand Central Market Bazaar, featuring handmade goods, clothing, jewelry and vintage sunglasses, on the lower level.

Oldest Flower Market
The Original Los Angeles Flower Market
754 Wall St.

W hile most of L.A. is still sleeping, The Original Los Angeles Flower Market comes to life in the six-block Flower District of downtown Los Angeles. Growers and vendors—many of them third-generation flower dealers—arrive in the early morning hours to sell their flowers and plants to their trade customers, usually florists, wedding planners, designers, and other merchants. Later in the day, the public is welcome to shop for flowers, vases, and gifts.

The market began informally in the early 1900s, when Los Angeles-area flower farmers traveled to the downtown produce market to sell their flowers. In 1905, Vawter Carnation Fields opened the first dedicated flower market on Spring Street in Downtown L.A. By 1910, local Japanese American farmers organized a flower market, which they incorporated in 1912. It became known as the Southern California Flower Market.

Inspired by the Japanese American growers, a group of 30 European American growers founded the American Florists' Exchange in 1919. Two years later, the group officially incorporated as American Florists' Exchange, Ltd., doing business as The Los Angeles Flower Market. As both major flower markets grew and prospered in the early 1920s, they relocated to more spacious quarters on the 700 block of South Wall Street.

The decades that followed brought innovation and growth,

as advances in the areas of horticulture and greenhouse technologies, refrigeration, transportation, and communications made the floral industry a global enterprise.

In 2011, The Original Los Angeles Flower Market transformed its main facility into a modern, solar-powered showcase for the floral offerings, grown in over a dozen different countries. In 1996, the flower market opened its doors to the general public.

Today, The Original Los Angeles Flower Market's 50 member vendors offer more than 125 different varieties of cut flowers that include azaleas, lilies, roses, China mums, carnations, and cherry blossoms, plus an impressive portfolio of related foliage and floral accessories. The market is the largest and most successful wholesale floral district in the entire United States.

The Original Los Angeles Flower Market has a rooftop parking structure between 7th and 8th sts. on the west side of San Julian St.

The Original Los Angles Flower Market has over 125 different varieties of cut flowers in addition to floral accessories.

OLDEST MEXICAN MARKETPLACE
OLVERA STREET

845 N Alameda St.

I f it wasn't for wealthy socialite Christina Sterling, Olvera
Street probably wouldn't be the bustling Mexican
marketplace it is today. While walking along El Pueblo Plaza
in 1926, she was shocked by the dilapidated condition of L.A.'s
oldest area.

Originally called Wine Street or Vine Street (due to its
location near vineyards), it was renamed Olvera in 1877 after
the county's first judge, Augustin Olvera, who lived on the
street. But by the turn of the century, once-grand homes and
buildings fell in disrepair.

The historic area was now a hideaway for prostitutes and
street crime. She saw a condemnation notice from city health
officials stating that the circa 1818 Avila Adobe was slated for
demolition. Knowing that Avila Adobe was the oldest house
in Los Angeles, she began to raise money to repair it and
surrounding buildings.

But she had loftier goals. Her dream was to create a Mexican
marketplace near the Avila Adobe where people could learn
about Los Angeles' Spanish and Mexican heritage. It was
through her efforts that many of the historic buildings around
the plaza were saved.

Olvera Street is a lively open-air Mexican Marketplace with cafes and vendors.

She invited merchants to sell their wares and artifacts, and to celebrate their fiestas as they would in Mexico. Olvera Street officially debuted as a pedestrian-only marketplace on Easter Sunday, April 20, 1930. Since then, Olvera Street has been a festive marketplace lined with Mexican shops and eateries serving tasty tacos, taquitos, enchiladas, and other traditional fare. Strolling mariachis and various events add to the festive ambiance.

The Olvera Street Merchants Association Foundation and El Pueblo host traditional events, which include The Blessing of the Animals, Día de los Muertos, and Las Posadas, a nine-day procession depicting the journey of Mary and Joseph to Bethlehem. Other events, like Fiestas Patrias or Cinco de Mayo, may be hosted by El Pueblo.

OLDEST OUTDOOR MURAL
AMÉRICA TROPICAL
125 Paseo De La Plaza

After artist David Alfaro Siqueiros was forced to leave Mexico for radical political militancy, he arrived in Los Angeles in 1932. He was commissioned by the La Plaza Art Center to paint an idealized tropical scene on a second-story exterior wall of the Italian Hall in downtown's Olvera Street. Instead, he painted an 80- by 18-foot mural depicting Maya ruins, an overgrown jungle, armed revolutionary soldiers, a crucified Indian figure, and an American eagle looming overhead.

When the mural was unveiled on October 9, 1932, it was immediately controversial for its political statement on US imperialism in Latin America. By 1938, the entire mural was whitewashed, and remained under layers of paint for the next 30 years. Around 1968 the mural began to slowly reappear as years of neglect, smog, and sun caused the paint to peel away.

In 1988, the Getty Conservation Institute collaborated with the City of Los Angeles to conserve *América Tropical*. Conservators agreed that because of the mural's severe deterioration, "it should be stabilized and conserved in its current state" instead of trying to restore the color. In addition, a protective shelter for the mural and a viewing platform for the public were constructed.

Eighty years after its creation, *América Tropical* was unveiled on October 9, 2012. The faded mural can be seen from a

Top left: *Photo of* América Tropical *in the Interpretive Center.*

Top right: América Tropical *Mexican artist David Alfaro Siqueiros's mural was considered controversial by conservatives because of its political message.*

Bottom left: América Tropical *sign in Interpretive Center.*

viewing platform at the América Tropical Interpretive Center, located in El Pueblo de Los Angeles Historical Monument.

The center, which also displays a replica of the mural in black and white, is dedicated to the life and legacy of Siqueiros, who completed three murals while in L.A. The most significant was his second mural—*América Tropical*, the first large-scale mural painted on an exterior wall and the only mural by Siqueiros in the US still in its original location.

The América Tropical Interpretive Center is located on the first floor of the Eastlake Victorian-style Sepulveda House, built in 1887 by Señora Eloisa Martinez de Sepulveda. The original structure included two commercial businesses and three residences. It's currently a preserved museum. 12 Olvera St.

Oldest Bakery
Phoenix Bakery
969 N Broadway

O n weekends, there's a line out the door for the family-run Phoenix Bakery, situated in the north end of Chinatown. But even during the week, the place is bustling with customers buying the bakery's signature strawberry cream cake, almond cookies, sugar butterflies, and other sweets reflecting various ethnic specialties.

The bakery was founded in 1938 by Chinese immigrants Fung Chow (F.C.) Chan and his wife, Wai Hing, on Broadway Street in downtown L.A. as a gathering place for the community. Using family recipes, the bakery produced traditional Chinese almond cookies, wintermelon pastries, seasonal moon cakes, and other pastries.

When F. C.'s brother, Lun, joined the bakery, he introduced a fresh strawberry whipped cream cake. But it wasn't until the 1970s that Phoenix became a popular bakery. With business flourishing in 1977, the Chan family moved from Chinatown's Central Plaza around the corner to a custom-built bakery on Broadway that remains their current location.

Today, the bakery is owned and managed by the second generation of the family: CEO Kathryn Chan Ceppi, her two younger brothers, Ken and Kelly Chan, and first cousin, Youlen Chan, who runs the kitchen. Their staff includes a baker who's been in the Phoenix kitchen for 50 years.

A Chinatown staple, Phoenix Bakery is known for its strawberry cream cake.

Ceppi and her brothers and cousins have worked in the bakery from the time they were little until they graduated from college. The boys worked in the kitchen, and Ceppi bagged fortune cookies and helped her dad with payroll. "He made me punch in and out too. He paid me a whopping 99 cents an hour," she said, laughing.

Around 2016, they considered closing the bakery. The second generation were busy professionals. "But our aunt said, 'it's your parents' legacy. They put you through school,'" said Ken Chan.

They agreed to keep Phoenix operating. "My brothers called me back, and said they needed a female here and a different perspective on things," said Ceppi, a retired pediatric occupational therapist. Five years ago she returned to the bakery to organize it and plan for the future. However, the bakery is in another transitional state, because none of their kids—the next generation—plan to take over. Fortunately, the family owns the property and has some options, said Ceppi.

The visionary F.C. Chan opened Phoenix Bakery in L.A.'s New Chinatown, which debuted in 1938 after the first Chinatown was razed to make way for Los Angeles Union Station. He also co-founded Cathay Bank, in 1962, and East West Federal Savings & Loan, in 1973, to serve Asian immigrants. Cathay Bank is the oldest Chinese American bank in Southern California.

Greater
Los Angeles Area

OLDEST CEMETERY
EVERGREEN CEMETERY
204 N Evergreen Ave.

A lthough the cemetery was established on August 23, 1877, it contains graves from the 1830s, before there was an official cemetery in Los Angeles.

Back then, families would bury the bodies of their loved ones in their backyards. After Evergreen Cemetery was established, families reburied the bodies in the cemetery.

With over 300,000 interments, the cemetery is one of the largest in L.A. Dozens of prominent L.A. figures (including the Lankershims and Van Nuyses) have been buried at Evergreen, which has a historic stone chapel for memorial services. The cemetery also contains a memorial for the 442nd Infantry Regimental Combat Unit of Japanese American soldiers.

When the cemetery was first established, it was segregated by ethnicity. There were separate sections for African Americans, and early residents of Japanese, Chinese, Mexican, and Armenian descent, in addition to members of the Jewish faith. The section near First and Lorena streets was a potter's field, where unclaimed bodies were buried.

The Chinese community, which was the sole ethnic group required to pay $10 for burials, was only allowed to bury its dead in a corner of the potter's field. That prompted the construction of a shrine on the site in 1888. The community purchased land on

Evergreen Cemetery contains graves from the 1830s.

First Street and Eastern Avenue in 1922 and relocated most of the remains to the new Chinese Cemetery.

In1992, the Chinese Historical Society of Southern California purchased the shrine and its plot of land. It was later declared a Los Angeles Historic-Cultural Monument.

The original location of the Chinese graves in the potter's field was discovered in 2005. Construction workers unearthed the remains of 174 people while excavating First Street for the extension of the Gold Line railway.

A memorial wall and meditation garden were dedicated near the Chinese shrine in 2010.

Adjacent to Evergreen Cemetery is the Los Angeles County Crematorium and Cemetery. Each year, about 1,700 homeless and unidentified persons are cremated and buried in a single grave. 3301 E 1st St.

Oldest Park
Elysian Park
929 Academy Rd.

As the oldest public park and the second-largest after Griffith Park, Elysian Park is an oasis of wilderness that snakes through the predominately low-income neighborhood of the same name. A small portion of the park falls in Echo Park.

Spanning about 600 acres, the park has playgrounds, picnic areas, and miles of hiking trails with viewpoints. It's also home to the Los Angeles Police Academy and Barlow Respiratory Hospital.

The 600-acre Elysian Park is adjacent to Dodger Stadium and wraps through a residential neighborhood.

Long before it became a dedicated city park, the area was home to the Yang-Na Indians and Chumash Indians. Later, in 1849, the land (known as Rock Quarry Hills) was nearly auctioned to produce city revenue. Instead, Rock Quarry Hills (named for the stone mined in the area) was withdrawn from public auction and reserved for public use.

The Los Angeles City Council dedicated Rock Quarry Hills as a city park and renamed it Elysian Park on April 5,1886. The name Elysian is derived from the Greek word "paradise."

Over the years, park boundaries shifted and were cut away or lost to landslides. A large portion of the park was turned over to the police department for an academy. In 1940, 30 acres were chopped away for the Pasadena Freeway, and another 30-acre parcel was ceded to the Los Angeles Dodgers in 1959.

Yet, Elysian Park survives as a slice of paradise in an urban setting.

Adjacent to the park is Dodger Stadium, built in 1962 and home of the Los Angeles Dodgers baseball team. Just north of Dodger Stadium, the Chavez Ravine Arboretum is the oldest arboretum in Southern California. Founded in 1893 by the Los Angeles Horticultural Society, the arboretum features over 100 varieties of trees from all over the world. Free admission. 929 Academy Rd.

OLDEST BOTTLED SODA SHOP

GALCO'S OLD WORLD GROCERY
GALCO'S SODA POP STOP

5702 York Blvd.

L ouis Nese and his son John had to agree to disagree in order to keep their family business running. Louis (who has since passed) and John had a different vision for Galco's Old World Grocery—also known as Galco's Soda Pop Stop.

Louis Nese became a partner in Galco's Imported Grocery between 1940 and 1943. The business was actually founded much earlier, in 1897, by the Galioto and Cortopassi families. Nese and his wife took over in 1955 and moved the grocery from downtown L.A. to Highland Park, where they sold

Galco's Soda Pop Stop owner John Nese stocks his store with over 750 different kinds of old-time sodas.

imported Italian goods and made deli sandwiches. The Blockbuster Italian sandwich, made with sourdough bread and Molinari cold cuts, became a became a best-selling item.

John Nese recalls going to work with his dad one summer when he was about eight years old. "Boy, was I in heaven. I had a Blockbuster sandwich and a soda every day," said John Nese, whose passion for soda dates to his summer

camp days when he would dream of hooking up the natural, bubbling spring water, adding syrup, and siphoning it to his school's drinking fountains.

When grocery sales began dipping in the 1990s, John Nese starting stocking the shelves with smaller brands of soda by

Galco's is a family business that started as an Italian Grocery and evolved into a specialty soda pop shop.

independent bottlers, much to the dismay of his dad. But with John's knack for finding old-time bottled sodas, business began picking up. Still, Louis Nese wasn't confident, and quietly encouraged their bookkeeper to find another job.

She didn't, because Galco's was thriving. John Nese started with about 100 bottled sodas, and now carries over 750 sodas from around the world that are not found in large chain stores. Galco's aisles are filled with a wide selection of unique and old-time favorites that include Moxie Original Elixer (originally served as "nerve" food in 1884), Hollywood Shirley Temple, Faygo Orange, Frostie Root Beer, and Lemmy Sparkling Lemonade (from 1939).

In addition to sodas, Galco's sells old-fashioned candy, wine, and craft beer. Though sodas and candy have replaced grocery items, Galco's has retained its deli and still makes the popular Blockbuster sandwich.

In 2013, Nese introduced the Soda Creation Station, where customers can craft their own sodas, selecting from over 100 syrups and choosing carbonation strength.

OLDEST MUSEUM
SOUTHWEST MUSEUM
234 Museum Dr.

It's a short, but steep, drive to the hilltop location of the Southwest Museum, home to Native American artifacts, in the Mount Washington neighborhood. Built in a mission revival style, the 12-acre campus houses a museum, library, and archive.

Founder Charles Lummis was asked to start the Southwest Society by the Archeological Institute of America in 1903. While the Southwest Museum's Mount Washington campus was formed in 1907, technically making it the oldest museum, it didn't open its doors until 1914. The Southwest Museum was part of Lummis's vision to make Los Angeles the center of art and culture.

Lummis chose the site in the traditional territory of the Gabriellno/Tongva Indians, high on a hill. Museum legend claims that Lummis believed one had to walk for knowledge. Fortunately for visitors, a tunnel and elevator were added in 1919-1920, making it much easier to reach the hilltop museum.

To accommodate the growing research collection, the Braun Research Library was built in 1977. Although the museum attracted visitors from around the world, it still suffered from low attendance and financial difficulties, leading to the merger with the nearby Autry Museum of Western Heritage in 2003.

Following the merger, the Autry was renamed the Autry Museum of the American West and initiated a conservation program to save and protect the Southwest's collections.

Although the Southwest Museum merged with the Autry, it's still located on its original site. The ground floor contains changing exhibits of Native American artifacts, while the lower level traces Lummis's stories and journeys. The outdoor terrace and garden offer panoramic views of the Arroyo Seco and downtown L.A.

The Mission Revival-style Southwest Museum contains exhibits of Native American artifacts.

The Southwest Museum is on the National Register of Historical Places as well as the California Register of Historic Places. It's also listed as a City of Los Angeles Historic-Cultural Monument.

In the late 1800s and early 1900s, Charles Fletcher Lummis built a Craftsman-style stone house in the northeastern section of the city, bordering Arroyo Seco. It's known as El Alisal, or "alder grove" in Spanish. 200 E Ave. 43.

Oldest Library
Vermont Square Branch Library
1201 W 48th St.

A manifestation of Andrew Carnegie's philanthropy, the Vermont Square Branch Library is situated in a small park on a quiet residential street. It was the earliest of six branch libraries, constructed with a $210,000 gift.

When the library opened on March 1, 1913, hundreds of people crowded into the library, excited to have what they considered a luxury in their neighborhood. The 8,000-square-foot library was built (at a cost of $38,466) in an Italian Renaissance style with a red-tiled roof and a cream-colored glazed brick and white tile exterior.

The librarian's desk is made of marble and wood. The library contains a young adults' room, children's area, an open reading room, and an auditorium. (Hanging in the children's room is a drawing of a young neighborhood girl, Alicia, by artist Leo Politi from 1972. She later returned for the library's 100th anniversary.)

The library was built to accommodate 16,000 books, but

opened with only 2,000 new books on hand. However, a "motion picture projection

The Vermont Square Branch Library was the first of six branch libraries built with a $210,000 grant by Andrew Carnegie.

machine" was donated to the library in 1917, and made its debut presenting the motion picture *The Prince and the Pauper* to a packed house.

The Vermont Square Branch Library children's room features a drawing by artist Leo Politi of a young neighborhood girl.

Over the years, the library served many purposes. A local exemption board set up its command post at the library during World War I, administering the selective draft for 20 months.

The library's service continued during World War II, when it became a Red Cross casualty center and an air raid shelter. It also operated as the Central Region library headquarters from 1949 to 1978.

The building closed for renovation in 1990 and reopened in May 1996. In June 1983, the Vermont Square Branch was designated a Historic-Cultural Monument by the Los Angeles Cultural Heritage Commission.

The Los Angeles Public Library has 72 branch libraries throughout the city. The crown jewel is the Richard J. Riordan Central Library, also known as Los Angeles Central Library, in downtown L.A. Built in 1926, the eight-story builing contains more than 10 million items. The rotunda's walls feature murals depicting California history. The building was added to the National Register of Historic Places in 1970.

OLDEST NATURAL HISTORY MUSEUM
NATURAL HISTORY MUSEUM OF LOS ANGELES COUNTY
900 W Exposition Blvd.

Although the museum wasn't the first documented museum in L.A., it was the first to open its doors to the public. When it officially opened on November 6, 1913, it was called the Museum of History, Science, and Art (the name changed several times throughout the years).

Located in Exposition Park, the museum was founded by the Los Angeles County government, the Historical Society of Southern California, the Cooper Ornithological Club, the Southern California Academy of Sciences, and the Fine Arts League.

From its beginning, the museum played an important role in L.A.'s history. As fossil excavations accelerated in the early 1900s, the museum received exclusive digging rights by 1913. Many of the fossils in the La Brea area filled the Natural Science Hall by 1914.

In the early 1930s, the museum was the first facility to collect early motion picture artifacts. Collections include Lon Chaney's makeup case from *Phantom of the Opera*, Scarlett O' Hara's barbecue dress

from *Gone with the Wind*, and Fred Astaire's tap shoes.

The T.rex growth series is the centerpiece of the museum's Dinosaur Hall exhibition, which features two floors of mounted skeletons, over 300 fossils, and a Dinosaur Lab. Photo courtesy of the Natural History Museums of Los Angeles County

Over the years, the museum's history, science, and art collections outgrew the 1913 building, which was expanded several times starting in 1925. The art component of the museum and the art collections split from the museum to form the Los Angeles County Museum of Art in 1961. A few years later, around 1970, the museum's name was changed to the Natural History Museum of Los Angeles County (NHM).

Today, the museum contains over 35 million specimens and artifacts, the largest natural and cultural history collection in the western United States. Exhibitions include the Age of Mammals, the Dinosaur Hall, Becoming Los Angeles, and the museum's famous dioramas. The Otis Booth Pavilion features the real skeleton of a California fin whale.

The museum continues to evolve. The upcoming NHM Commons, scheduled to open in 2023, will feature a multipurpose theater, a café, retail space, and a large community plaza.

The museum is part of a larger group of museums called the Natural History Museums of Los Angeles County, consisting of the Natural History Museum of Los Angeles County, the La Brea Tar Pits, and the William S. Hart Museum.

Situated by the museum, the seven-acre Exposition Park Rose Garden was unveiled in 1928 with over 15,000 rosebushes surrounding a central fountain. Today the garden—a popular place for weddings and other special events—has over 200 different varieties of plants and flowers. Listed on the National Register of Historic Places, the garden is closed to the public from January 1 to March 15 of each year for annual maintenance. 701 State Dr.

Oldest Automobile Dealership
Felix Chevrolet
3330 S Figueroa St.

At age 14, Darryl Holter was a little too old for cartoons, but he was familiar with Felix the Cat. Little did he know at the time the big role the famous cartoon character would play in his future business. Holter is owner of L.A.'s oldest dealership—Felix Chevrolet dealership, which gained fame for the large, three-sided sign featuring the iconic Felix the Cat.

But the story begins with Winslow B. Felix, who established Felix Chevrolet in 1921. He became friends with Pat Sullivan, one of the creators behind Felix the Cat. Since Winslow and the cat shared the same name, they decided to cross-market their brands. The dealership would market the cat and the cartoon character would promote the Felix Chevrolet dealership location.

Winslow died at age 46, when he was trampled by a horse in 1936. Nicholas Shammas purchased Felix Chevrolet in 1955 and moved it to the current site in 1957. Around 1959, a new freeway system was being built. To increase visibility to his dealership, Shammas commissioned a giant, three-sided neon sign to be erected at the dealership. The new, smiling Felix the Cat sign helped to put Felix Chevrolet on the map.

Meanwhile, Holter, who was married to Shammas's daughter, moved to L.A. in 1991. Holter joined the family business and used

Felix Chevrolet is a longtime automobile dealership long recognizable by the Felix the Cat sign.

Left: *Felix Chevrolet lot in the late 1960s, courtesy of the Felix Chevrolet Collection*

Right: *Felix Chevrolet lot in 2020, courtesy of Meridian-cmg*

his organizational skills to band with local property owners and clean up the deteriorating district to make it clean and safe again.

The Internet has changed the new car industry considerably in the last 20 years. Prior to that, people would visit a dealership unsure of what they wanted and would spend hours talking with a salesman. "Nowadays, people go online and by the time they contact the dealership they know what they want," said Holter (who wrote a song, "Don't Touch My Chevy").

But one thing hasn't changed for Felix Chevrolet. Holter said people come from all over to see the sign. And there are plenty of Felix Chevrolet vehicle plates to prove it.

Built in 1855, Figueroa is one of the oldest, and grew to be one of the longest, streets in the city of L.A. Figueroa runs north to south for 22 unbroken miles, from Eagle Rock to San Pedro. Named for Jose Figueroa, former governor of Alta, California (1833-1835), the street's original segment lies between Pico and Exposition blvds.

OLDEST THEMED RESTAURANT
TAM O' SHANTER
2980 Los Feliz Blvd.

The Scottish-themed Tam O'Shanter restaurant is a gathering place for just about any occasion. From casual luncheons and family dinners to business meetings and special events, the restaurant serves as a go-to spot for locals.

It's been in the same location since 1922, when Walter Van de Kamp and Lawrence Frank, the founders of Van de Kamps Holland Dutch Bakeries and the Lawry's restaurant chain, commissioned architect and set designer Harry Oliver to build a storybook-style roadside restaurant. The restaurant opened as Montgomery's Country Inn.

In 1925, the restaurant was renamed Tam O'Shanter Inn after a Robert Burns poem. For years, the restaurant was a favorite lunch spot for Walt Disney and his animators, and many Hollywood

stars, including Mary Pickford, Douglas Fairbanks, and John Wayne.

The Tam O' Shanter's storybook-style architecture stands out on busy Los Feliz Boulevard.

The Scottish-themed Tam O'Shanter restaurant was a favorite lunch spot for Walt Disney and his animators.

Inside the dimly lit restaurant, Scottish medieval weapons, crests, kilts, tartans, and coats of arms adorn the walls from floor to ceiling. Menu mainstays include "Toad in a Hole," homemade potato chips, and the restaurant's signature prime rib dinner.

On the third Friday of each month, the restaurant turns one of its most historic rooms into a reservation-only speakeasy complete with live jazz, red lighting, tableside cocktails, and a separate entrance.

In 2018, the historic patio was brought back, 70 years after it had closed. That worked well during the pandemic, when indoor dining was prohibited.

Rumor has it that the Tam O' Shanter's design was used for Snow White's cottage or Pinocchio's Daring Journey ride at Disneyland.

Oldest Mexican Restaurant
El Cholo
1121 S Western Ave.

El Cholo feels like a cozy family home. Framed photos and family memorabilia are displayed throughout the various spaces and nooks added on throughout the years. Good smells come from the kitchen in the family-owned Mexican restaurant, which spans three generations. El Cholo has several locations (owned by various family members), but the original spot is on Western Avenue.

El Cholo's history began with Rosa and Alejandro Borquez, who opened the Sonora Cafe in 1923 (the name changed to El Cholo in 1925), specializing in Mexican dishes from Rosa's childhood in Sonora, Mexico. They bought 60-pound cheese wheels aged for one year, a tradition El Cholo continues.

Their daughter Aurelia and her husband, George Salisbury, opened their own El Cholo in 1926, a small space with just eight

stools and a hot top stove to heat tortillas and melt cheese enchiladas. In 1931 they moved El Cholo across the street to a two-bedroom home, transforming it into the current restaurant, now owned by their

El Cholo's walls are adorned by a large mural, photos, and various memorabilia.

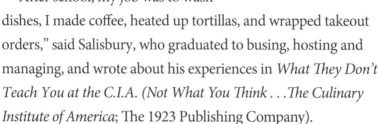

El Cholo has been serving authentic Mexican food in a homey environment since 1923.

son, Ron Salisbury, who began working at El Cholo at around age 12.

"After school, my job was to wash dishes, I made coffee, heated up tortillas, and wrapped takeout orders," said Salisbury, who graduated to busing, hosting and managing, and wrote about his experiences in *What They Don't Teach You at the C.I.A. (Not What You Think . . . The Culinary Institute of America*; The 1923 Publishing Company).

El Cholo's traditional Mexican menu includes original specialties like seasonal green corn tamales. For 75 years the corn was cut by hand with a knife, until 1998, when Ron Salisbury bought a machine that sped up the process. More menu favorites include a Taste of History: a plate with a cheese enchilada, rolled beef taco, chili relleno, pork tamale, Spanish rice, and beans.

From the beginning El Cholo was known for fresh food at fair prices. Salisbury said that before Jack Nicholson became famous, he would swing by for five-cent coffee and a 75-cent plate of tacos and beans.

Part of El Cholo's charm are the longtime employees. Joe Reina was chef for 53 years. And Elvira, a server for over 36 years, said her dad was a dishwasher at El Cholo. Not surprisingly, El Cholo treats its employees like family, proudly displaying a chart with an employee timeline in the lobby.

Owned by family members, El Cholo has locations in downtown L.A., Santa Monica, Anaheim Hills, Corona Del Mar, and La Habra.

1923

OLDEST STADIUM
LOS ANGELES MEMORIAL COLISEUM
3911 Figueroa St.

T he Los Angeles Memorial Coliseum, credited with helping to bring professional sports teams to the West Coast, represents L.A.'s transformation from a small city into a major metropolis in the early 20th century.

The Coliseum was commissioned in 1921 as a memorial to Los Angeles veterans of World War I, and it was rededicated to all veterans in 1968. The official groundbreaking ceremony took place on December 21, 1921, and work was completed on May 1, 1923, in the newly opened Exposition Park.

A few months later, on October 6, the first football game was played between the University of Southern California (USC) and Pomona College before 12,836 fans. The USC Trojans won 23-7. The Coliseum continues to serve as the home field for the USC Trojans.

Throughout the years, countless historic events have taken place in the Coliseum. It's the only facility in the world to have hosted two Olympic Games (1932 and 1984), two Super Bowls (I and VII) and one World Series (1959). It also was the site for the Los Angeles Dodgers before the baseball team moved to its own stadium. UCLA played football in the Coliseum from 1933 to 1981, before shifting to the Rose Bowl Stadium.

The 1932 Summer Olympic Games marked the first time that athletes were housed within an Olympic Village. Other rituals

The Los Angeles Memorial Coliseum has been the site for many sports and historic events. Photo courtesy of Los Angeles Tourism & Convention Board

debuted here, including the flying of the winning nations' flags and the addition of national anthems.

The Coliseum was the site for historic events, as well. During the 1960 Democratic Convention, John Kennedy and Lyndon Johnson delivered their acceptance speeches in the arena, and in 1987 Pope John Paul II addressed a crowd.

In August 2019, the Coliseum underwent a $315 million renovation, which included a new press box on the south side of the field, new seating, and updated amenities.

In 1984, the State of California and the United States Government declared the L.A. Coliseum a State and Federal Historical Landmark for its contribution to the history of California and the US.

The Los Angeles Memorial Coliseum is located in historic Exposition Park. Originally created as Agricultural Park in 1872, and renamed Exposition Park in 1913, the 160-acre urban park is also home to several museums, the Rose Garden, Banc of California Stadium, and EXPO Center. 700 Exposition Park Dr.

OLDEST FOSSIL DIG SITE
LA BREA TAR PITS
5801 Wilshire Blvd.

L ong before the snarling traffic along today's Wilshire Boulevard, mammoths, mastodons, saber-toothed cats, dire wolves, ground sloths, and other Ice Age animals roamed the area that evolved into bustling Los Angeles. You can still see traces of them at La Brea Tar Pits, where plants and animals from the last 50,000 years are still being discovered on-site nearly every day, making it the only active urban fossil dig site in the world.

Before it became an active dig site, humans used the asphalt for various uses. In 1828, the Rancho La Brea area was a Mexican Land Grant of over 4,400 acres given to Antonio Jose Rocha with the proviso that pueblo residents could have access to as much asphalt as they needed.

As L.A. grew, the Rancho was eventually subdivided and developed. The last owner, George Allan Hancock, recognized the scientific importance of the fossils found in the asphaltic deposits and donated 23 acres of the ranch to the County of Los Angeles with the stipulation that the park be preserved, and the fossils properly exhibited. Hancock Park was created in 1924.

The Tar Pits are considered by many scientists to be among the greatest finds in modern history. The pungent tar—actually pools of asphalt—has been seeping up from a natural subterranean petroleum spring underneath L.A. for several millennia. The tar, often covered with dust, leaves, or water, preserved the bones of trapped animals.

Left: *Specimens are prepared in the see-through Fossil Lab at the George C. Page Museum at La Brea Tar Pits.*

Right: *Fossils are still discovered nearly every day at the Tar Pits.*

It's free to watch excavators carve and dig out fossils from the asphalt at outdoor dig sites. There's an admission fee to enter the on-site George C. Page Museum, which contains exhibits and a see-through Fossil Lab where scientists sort microfossils, clean mammoth tusks, and do other tasks.

Galleries feature the fossils of Ice Age animals as well as the tiny, but scientifically significant, microfossils of insects, plants, mammals, and reptiles. Among the exhibits is a barrel of tar that visitors can stir to get a feel for what it was like to get stuck in the gooey mass.

The only prehistoric human remains uncovered at La Brea Tar Pits (Pit 10) were those of La Brea Woman, found in 1914, and estimated to be about 9,000 years old. Based on the partial skeleton and skull that were excavated, she likely was about four feet eight to four feet ten inches tall and between 18 and 24 years old. She consumed stone-ground foods, based on an analysis of her remaining teeth. Nearby was a broken grinding stone, and her fractured skull suggested a blow to the head may have killed her.

OLDEST BOWLING ALLEY
HIGHLAND PARK BOWL
5621 N Figueroa St.

I n the midst of the country's Prohibition (1920-1933), Highland Park Bowl debuted in 1927 and served the neighborhood as a multipurpose pharmacy and social gathering place. The building housed a pharmacy, music store, bowling alley, recreation area, and various doctor offices that were located on the second story.

Since the US Treasury Department authorized physicians to write prescriptions for medicinal alcohol, Highland Park Bowl customers could obtain a prescription upstairs—the going rate for a whiskey prescription was about $3—head downstairs to fill the prescription (and their glass), and enjoy drinking and bowling. In 1932-33, the music store in the building obtained a permit for live music performances.

Meanwhile, the Highland Park community was prospering with a growing theater and arts scene in the 1930s. The Anderson Brothers were commissioned to paint a mural at Highland Park Bowl depicting the community's surrounding scenery.

In 1966, Joseph "Mr. T" Teresa purchased the property and renamed it Mr. T's Bowl, concealing the original design and mural and transforming it to a mid-century style venue. When bowling alleys began to diminish in the 1980s, the space was

From its beginning, Highland Park Bowl has been a fun place to bowl and imbibe.

The prohibition-era High Park Bowl has been restored with vintage elements.

transformed into a music venue and the eight lanes were covered by a large curtain. "Mr. T" passed away in 2005; and 1933 Group acquired the bowling alley in 2014.

"My goal was to take the bones of the structure back to its original incarnation," said 1933 Group co-owner and lead designer, Bobby Green.

To restore the place to its original decor, 1933 Group peeled away years of remodeled elements to reveal the Spanish Revival aesthetic of the building's façade and structure. During this process, elements including the bow truss architecture, skylights, and mural painted by the Anderson Brothers were uncovered. This mural is now the backdrop to the lanes.

The decor incorporates a collection of vintage pieces from the alley's past. Pinsetters were transformed into chandeliers, bowling machines were repurposed as bar shelves, and multiple display cabinets showcase recovered bowling trinkets, pennants, and artifacts spanning the building's timeline.

Brunswick pin machines, sourced from the 1980s, were refurbished and remain exposed so that people can watch the workings of the machines as they bowl, eat, drink and listen to live music. Just like in the old days.

During the bowling alley's renovation, 1933 Group made some discoveries: an original 1930s candy machine with candy still inside. "The biggest surprise was finding out that Highland Park Bowl was the oldest surviving alley in the west," said 1933 Group co-owner Bobby Green.

OLDEST FARMERS MARKET
THE ORIGINAL FARMERS MARKET
6333 W 3rd St.

With over 100 merchants that include ethnic restaurants, bakeries, candymakers, a fish market, and specialty foods at the corner of iconic 3rd and Fairfax, The Original Farmers Market is popular with tourists, locals, and celebrities. (In fact, by the 1950s the market was a celebrity hotspot with special appearances by Marilyn Monroe and The Beatles.) It's a fun place to enjoy a meal, shop for gifts and attend seasonal events.

Before the market, the space was farmland. Wealthy landowner Arthur Fremont Gilmore owned a dairy herd and later oil derricks until L.A.'s boundaries expanded to surround his property. The new boundaries no longer permitted oil derricks on a large scale.

The land remained vacant until the 1930s, when entrepreneurs

The Original Farmers Market is an iconic gathering place at 3rd and Fairfax. Photo courtesy of The Original Farmers Market

Fred Beck and Roger Dahlhjelm approached Gilmore's son Earl Bell (E. B.) Gilmore with an idea for a village at the corner of 3rd Street and Fairfax Avenue, where local farmers could sell their fresh goods. E. B. Gilmore agreed, and in July 1934 a dozen farmers and a few other merchants parked their trucks at the corner and sold their fresh produce from the back of the trucks. Vendors paid 50 cents a day in rent.

Three months after it opened, farmers and merchants began moving into permanent stalls. Magee's Kitchen, the first restaurant at the market and only original tenant remaining, is among the purveyors who have become L.A. institutions in their own right. Bennett's Ice Cream has been scooping ice cream since 1963, Du-Par's has been serving buttermilk hotcakes since 1938, and Marconda's is L.A.'s oldest standing meat market, dating to 1941. For over 25 years Monsieur Marcel Gourmet Market and Bistro has been offering imported goods and authentic French cuisine. The Clock Tower became an icon of the Farmers Market in 1948.

In 1991, the Los Angeles City Council declared Farmers Market a Historic-Cultural Monument. In 2014, Farmers Market opened another location at Los Angeles International Airport Terminal 5.

The Original Farmers Market is a bustling place. It's a good idea to arrive before 11.a.m. to explore, dine and shop. For a fee, there's also a 2.5-hour Melting Pot Food Tour that includes the market's history and tastings at bakeries, candy shops, a gourmet market (with one of L.A.'s finest cheese counters), and more.

Oldest Neighborhood Bookstore
Chevalier's Books
133 N Larchmont Blvd.

In 1939, Joe Chevalier and his first wife, Marguerite (she later died in 1953) bought Rene's Rental Library, where books were renting for three cents a day. *Grapes of Wrath* was on the bestseller list when Chevalier's first opened for business in 1940. They kept the rental rate but changed the name to Chevalier's Book Store.

Joe Chevalier was working for Carnation Co. at the time, and couldn't work at the bookstore full-time until 1945. The store changed locations on Larchmont Boulevard twice and expanded to include stationery and greeting cards, and an art gallery.

Early on, Chevalier established a reputation for personalized service and a willingness to track down hard-to-find books. As a collector of rare books, Chevalier was known to help customers find whatever books they wanted.

In 1990, Joe Chevalier sold the store to Filis Winthrop and two co-owners. Though her various co-owners changed over time, Winthrop remained an owner for about 25 years, until she sold the struggling bookstore to Bert Deixler and Darryl Holter in 2014.

Holter said they saw potential in the store and bought it for three reasons: the foot traffic and surrounding community, good

Chevalier's Books is a compact independent bookstore in trendy Larchmont Village.

demographics composed of affluent, educated people, and the store's legacy.

"Independent bookstores have survived by maintaining close ties with the community. Our books reflect the community: that's one of the characteristics of our store," said Holter.

"Amazon's strategy is to undercut competitors," said Holter. So Chevalier's does what Amazon can't. In addition to finding books that customers request, the bookstore hosts author signings, children's readings, book clubs, and other events to bring customers in and connect with them.

Chevalier's sits in the middle of a trendy shopping street with sidewalk cafes and laid-back shops in the charming nook of Larchmont Village, a half-square-mile neighborhood in Hancock Park. It was established in 1891 and developed in the 1920s.

OLDEST DRIVE-THROUGH HAMBURGER STAND

IN-N-OUT BURGER

13850 Francisquito Ave., Baldwin Park

I n an era when carhops brought burgers and shakes to the windows of motorists, Harry and Esther Snyder launched the first drive-through hamburger stand in a 10-foot-square space at Francisquito and Garvey avenues in Baldwin Park. It featured a unique two-way speaker box so customers could order food from their cars.

From the beginning, In-N-Out made it a point to offer a simple menu with freshly made, quality food. Hamburgers are made to order, potatoes are peeled and diced by hand for French fries, and shakes are made with real ice cream.

In the hamburger stand's early days, Harry would visit the meat and produce markets to pick out fresh ingredients, which he prepared by hand. His wife handled all the restaurant's accounting from their home around the corner. As the business prospered, they hired associates (employees are still called associates).

In 1954, the logo changed from "No Delay" to the iconic In-N-Out arrow. By 1958 the restaurant had five locations in the San Gabriel Valley. Fountain drinks replaced bottles, and included Pepsi Cola®, Nesbitt Orange and Hires Root Beer. A 12-ounce cup (without lid) cost 10 cents.

Animal-style burgers were introduced in 1961. These mustard-fried patties with extra sauce and toppings are still made, but not on the official menu. Next, the popular double-double debuted in 1963, becoming part of the regular menu.

By 1973, In-N-Out had 13 drive-through restaurants in Los Angeles County. In 1974, In-N-Out started a tradition of grilling burgers for the Tournament of Roses Parade in Pasadena, feeding tournament bands at Band Fest, and football teams at Team Feed.

In-N-Out was the first drive through hamburger stand. Photo courtesy of In-N-Out Hamburgers

The Snyders' sons Rich and Guy Snyder (who have since passed away) took over as president and vice president, respectively, in 1976. Dining rooms were added in 1979 to the restaurants as the company expanded its locations. The California-based burger stand currently has locations in California, Nevada, Arizona, Utah, Texas, Oregon, and Colorado.

In 2014, a replica of the first In-N-Out opened to the public for viewing and photos. 13752 Francisquito Ave., Baldwin Park.

Oldest Trains
Travel Town Museum
5200 Zoo Dr.

Visitors to Travel Town Museum can ride a 16-gauge miniature train and climb aboard historic locomotives in a train yard. Located near the Los Angeles Zoo in Griffith Park, Travel Town's collection includes 40-plus, full-size locomotives, freight cars, cabooses, passenger trains, motorcars, and interurbans. Travel Town preserves the railroad heritage of the western United States and shows how the railroads aided Southern California's development.

Travel Town was the vision of Charley Atkins, a Recreation and Parks employee, and a handful of rail enthusiast friends. It was the late 1940s, and the plan was to add a steam locomotive by the existing Griffith Park miniature railroad ride, and to create a place where kids could imagine themselves as engineers.

Travel Town houses a collection of vintage locomotives and old-time vehicles including a Carnation milk truck.

Since the City of Los Angeles Harbor Department had two little engines destined for scrap, it seemed like a good time to create a transportation attraction. Atkins, with the enthusiastic support of former Recreation and Parks Department General

Travel Town contains a collection of vintage locomotives and vehicles.

Manager George Hjelte and Superintendent of Recreation William Frederickson, initiated contacts with major railroads in California to determine what equipment they might be willing to donate. At that time, the steam locomotive era was drawing to a close, so Atkins got a good response.

Travel Town was dedicated on December 14, 1952.

Travel Town is among many attractions located within the 4,200-acre Griffith Park. The park dates to 1896, when Colonel Griffith J. Griffith and his wife, Mary Agnes Christine (Tina), donated over 3,000 acres to the City of L.A. for recreational use. Griffith Park is home to the Griffith Observatory, Los Angeles Zoo, Equestrian Center, Griffith Merry-Go-Round, Greek Theater, Autry Museum of the American West, Griffith Park Southern Railroad, Griffith Park Pony Rides, and hiking trails.

HOLLYWOOD

Oldest Continuously Operating Hollywood Studio

Paramount Pictures

5515 Melrose Ave.

Lights, camera, action—Paramount has been on the forefront of moviemaking since Hollywood's earliest history. Because it involves the merger of numerous companies, Paramount uses the start date of all of them as several "anniversaries," earning it the title of the longest-operating and only remaining major studio in Hollywood.

It began with Adolph Zukor's full-length drama *Queen Elizabeth* and Famous Players in 1912, the same year that W. W. Hodkinson founded Paramount's distributing company. Four years later, Famous Players merged with the Jesse L. Lasky Company and eventually consolidated with Paramount. All three companies became known as Paramount Pictures.

In 1926, the Paramount Pictures studio lot was built on 26 acres with four sound stages at a cost of $1 million. From the 1930s to 1950s the studio was successful, with classics featuring Bing Crosby and Cecil B. DeMille.

In the mid-1960s, Paramount ventured into television. The lot acquired Desilu Television Studios from Lucille Ball in 1967

Paramount Pictures has a long, complex history in Hollywood.

and expanded the lot. From 2000 to the present, Paramount has remained a leader in the film industry and production technology.

Paramount Pictures' long roster of movies includes *The Godfather* (1972), *Forrest Gump* (1994), *Titanic* (1997), *Shrek* (2004), and *Once Upon a Time in Hollywood* (2019).

Proximity to Paramount made Musso & Frank Grill a favorite watering hole for actors, writers, directors, and studio executives. It also had the town's first pay phone. Frank Toulet opened the restaurant as Frank's Café on September 27, 1919. He partnered with Joseph Musso, they changed the name to Musso & Frank Grill, and sold the restaurant to Joseph Carissimi and John Mosso. Primarily known for its steaks and signature martinis, the restaurant exudes an Old Hollywood ambiance. It's owned and operated by Mosso's three granddaughters and their children. 6667 Hollywood Blvd.

Oldest Frank Lloyd Wright House

Hollyhock House

4800 Hollywood Blvd.

Aline Barnsdall, an oil heiress and patron of the arts who traveled extensively, bought a 36-acre property atop Olive Hill in 1919 to create a destination for the arts in Los Angeles. She commissioned architect Frank Lloyd Wright to design the house.

Taking advantage of L.A.'s mild climate, Wright designed a garden-style house that integrates the indoors with outdoor gardens and living spaces. Numerous doors and windows allow for cross breezes, while terraces offer city and garden views. He incorporated Barnsdall's favorite flower—the hollyhock—into the design throughout the house in windows, columns, concrete friezes, and furniture. Hollyhocks were also planted around the house.

Wright designed the home's entrance on the side, with formidable front doors that have a fortress feeling. The underlying tone was that guests had to be invited into this private space. Upon entering the home, there's an open floor plan that doesn't use doors and walls to divide rooms. Rather, a spindle screen separates the music room from the foyer. And steps down to the large living room, and up to the small dining room, define these spaces.

The Hollyhock House sits atop a hill in Barnsdall Park.

Wright's compression and release architectural concept moves people into rooms he wants them to inhabit. He reasoned the foyer doesn't need a high ceiling, but the spacious living room does. The room's focal point is the hearth, set back by a moat and topped by a skylight, exemplifying the four elements of water, fire, earth, and air. In the dining room, he designed a small, round table and just six chairs, believing that an intelligent conversation couldn't be held by more than six people.

But the house was never finished. Barnsdall rarely occupied the house, and Wright was working on a project in Japan. Barnsdall fired Wright, and construction was supervised by Wright's son Lloyd Wright and Rudolf Schindler. Since Barnsdall's vision for a theater mecca didn't come to fruition, she gifted 12 of the 36 acres to the City of Los Angeles in 1927. The city later finished construction.

The house was designated as a National Historic Landmark in 2007, and was inscribed as the first United Nations Educational, Scientific, and Cultural Organizaiton (UNESCO) World heritage Site in L.A.

Hollyhock House is located in the Barnsdall Art Park, which encompasses a city park as well as youth and adult art programs and classes. The park is dedicated to the memory of Aline's father, Theodore Barnsdall. 4800 Hollywood Blvd.

OLDEST AMPHITHEATER
JOHN ANSON FORD THEATRE
2580 Cahuenga Blvd. E

I t's easy to see why author Christine Wetherill Stevenson, an heiress to the Pittsburgh Paint fortune, chose the rugged Cahuenga Pass as the site for the future Ford Theatre and her production of *The Pilgrimage Play* in 1920.

The 1,200-seat, open-air theater, built with wooden seats, was tucked against the Hollywood Hills in the Santa Monica Mountains, providing a dramatic backdrop for her play, based on the four gospels according to the King James version of the Bible. The play was performed by professional actors every summer from 1920 to 1929, when the original theater burned in a fire.

The current Ford Theatre, which opened in 1931, was built on the same site. This time, however, it was built using poured concrete. Architect William Lee Woollett designed the theater in the style of ancient Judaic architecture to resemble the Jerusalem city gates.

The Pilgrimage Play resumed production until 1964. After the theater's site was deeded to the County of Los Angeles, a lawsuit forced the closure of the play due to the religious theme.

The Pilgrimage Theatre was renamed the John Anson Ford Theatre in 1976, in honor of the late Los Angeles County Supervisor's support of the arts.

The amphitheater remains among L.A.'s favorite venues for live summer performances of music, dance, film, and family

The Ford Theatre was built for Christine Wetherill Stevenson's The Pilgrimage Play. Photo courtesy of Los Angeles Philharmonic Archives

events that reflect L.A. communities. And the fact that no patron is more than 96 feet away from the stage means everyone has a good seat. The Ford's centennial season, which would have been commemorated in 2020, will be celebrated in 2022.

In December 2019, the Los Angeles Philharmonic Association took responsibility for The Ford, after it was assigned to the organization by the Los Angeles County Board of Supervisors. The Los Angeles Philharmonic—commonly called LA Phil—was founded by William Andrews Clark Jr., a philanthropist and amateur musician, who established it as the city's first permanent symphony orchestra in 1919. The orchestra performs or presents more than 250 concerts at the Frank Gehry-designed Walt Disney Concert Hall, The Ford, and the Hollywood Bowl.

Oldest Outdoor Concert Venue
Hollywood Bowl
2301 N Highland Ave.

An evening under the stars while catching a concert at the Hollywood Bowl is one of the most quintessential L.A. experiences. Especially since you can bring your own bottle of wine to the venue. Hosting the finest artists from all genres of music, the Hollywood Bowl is one of the largest natural amphitheaters in the world, with a seating capacity of nearly 18,000.

The Hollywood Bowl is situated in the Daisy Dell Canyon, which was the site for various performances in 1919 and 1920. The following year marked the first performance of the iconic Los Angeles Philharmonic–LA Phil– at the newly named

The Hollywood Bowl got its elliptical form in 1926. Photo courtesy of Los Angeles Philharmonic Archives

Hollywood Bowl for an Easter sunrise service. LA Phil returned the following year for Easter and to launch its summer-long musical festival (then called Symphonies Under the Stars), which began on July 11, 1922, and has run ever since.

The Hollywood Bowl hosts a variety of musical artists. Photo courtesy of Christina Mendelson

Back in its early days, the first spectators sat on temporary wooden benches to watch Alfred Hertz conduct the Los Angeles Philharmonic. In 1926, Pasadena architect and Rose Bowl designer Myron Hunt created an elliptical form for the Hollywood Bowl's seating amphitheater. His layout featured monumental stairways that reinforced the seating area's dramatic balloon shape.

Seating is much more comfortable today, with various options: bench seats, stadium-style seats with cup holders, and the popular box seats, ideal for groups of four or six, surrounded by wooden partitions. Renovations continued over the years, enhancing the Bowl with LED jumbo screens and an outdoor wine bar.

Located across from the Hollywood Bowl, the Hollywood Heritage Museum contains historical photos, props, documents, and other movie-related memorabilia from Hollywood's early film days. The museum is housed in the restored Lasky-DeMille barn where Cecil B. DeMille filmed The Squaw Man *(1914). 2100 N Highland Ave.*

OLDEST FAMOUS SIGN
HOLLYWOOD SIGN
Hollywood Hills

Among L.A.'s most cherished and photographed landmarks is the Hollywood sign. Perched on Mount Lee in the Hollywood Hills area of the Santa Monica Mountains, the 350-foot long sign spells out the name Hollywood in 45-foot-tall, white capital letters. Originally called the Hollywoodland sign, it was built in 1923 by then *Los Angeles Times* publisher Harry Chandler as a $21,000 billboard for his upscale Hollywoodland real estate development.

The original letters were 30 feet wide and about 43 feet tall, constructed of three-by-nine-foot metal squares rigged together by an intricate frame of scaffolding, pipes, wires, and telephone poles.

The sign featured 4,000 20-watt bulbs, spaced eight inches apart. A giant white dot (35 feet in diameter, with 20-watt lights on the perimeter) was constructed below the sign to catch the eye. At night the sign would flash: first "Holly" then "wood" and finally "land."

The sign was intended to last just a year and a half. But it became a famous tourist attraction and symbol for Hollywood, as well as a popular backdrop in many films and TV shows.

With the sign's deterioration in the 1940s, the developers sold it to the City of Los Angeles. In 1949, the Hollywood Chamber of Commerce and the City of Los Angeles Department of

Recreation and Parks partnered to repair the sign and shorten the name to simply Hollywood.

The sign has seen its share of vandalism. In 1973, pranksters changed the name to read "Hollyweed" and layer to "Holywood," commemorating a visit from Pope John II in 1987.

In 1978, the Hollywood sign underwent restoration that included the installation of a security system. The sign is protected and promoted by nonprofit The Hollywood Sign Trust.

While it's illegal to reach the sign, there are several trails that get close enough for good photos. The easiest way up is via the Mt. Hollywood Trail, which begins at the Charlie Turner Trailhead, accessible from the Griffith Observatory parking lot.

The Hollywood sign is the most photographed sign in L.A.

───────────────────────1927
OLDEST HOLLYWOOD HOTEL
THE HOLLYWOOD ROOSEVELT HOTEL
7000 Hollywood Blvd.

D ating to Hollywood's Golden Age, the Hollywood Roosevelt Hotel opened on May 15, 1927. Named for President Theodore Roosevelt, the hotel was financed by a group that included Douglas Fairbanks, Mary Pickford, and Sid Grauman. At the time, it cost $2.5 million to complete the 12-story building, which has 300 rooms and suites, a Spanish Colonial-style lobby and the Blossom Ballroom.

For generations, the hotel has welcomed VIPs. Marilyn Monroe lived at the for two years in a vintage 1950s cabana (now named the Marilyn Suite), at the time of her first professional magazine shoot, which took place at the hotel's pool.

Clark Gable and Carole Lombard stayed in the penthouse (at the time $5/night), which is also named for them. The 3,200-square-foot duplex, which has an outdoor deck, is tucked beneath the Roosevelt's iconic sign and has views of the Hollywood Hills and Hollywood sign.

In 1929, the Roosevelt's glamorous ballroom was the site of the first Academy Awards ceremony. A private dinner preceded the awards, which were presented in 12 categories in just 15 minutes. The 4,500-square-foot ballroom was recently renovated to its original grandeur with 25-foot-tall, LED-lighted ceilings, custom chandeliers, and original ceiling details.

The Hollywood Roosevelt Hotel, steeped in Hollywood history, was the site of the first Academy Awards ceremony. Photo courtesy of Los Angeles Tourism & Convention Board

In 1988, famed British painter David Hockney completed a multimillion-dollar mural on the bottom of the Tropicana Pool. Both the hotel and the pool have been designated Historic-Cultural Monuments by the city's Cultural Heritage Commission. The 1960's-style Tropicana pool was recently renovated.

In 1991, the Hollywood Roosevelt was designated Los Angeles Historic-Cultural Monument No. 545.

Nearby are two historic theaters built by Sid Grauman and Charles E. Toberman. The Pharaoh-themed Egyptian Theatre was built in 1922 for silent film classics. 6712 Hollywood Blvd. The TLC Theatre opened in 1927 and has been a site for red-carpet premieres. It was also the site for the Academy Awards ceremonies in the 1940s. The theater's forecourt features handprints and signatures of nearly 200 celebrities. 6925 Hollywood Blvd.

Oldest Cosmetic Building
Max Factor Building/The Hollywood Museum
1660 N Highland Ave.

Marilyn Monroe, Lucille Ball, and Rita Hayworth were among the first women transformed into Hollywood starlets by makeup artist Max Factor, a Polish immigrant.

Known as Hollywood's "makeup king," Max Factor created a cosmetic empire by inventing the tube lipstick, pancake makeup, color harmony (the precision use of makeup and shading), and a line of cosmetics for celebrities as well as housewives.

In 1928, he bought a glamorous, art deco-style building in Hollywood, although the opening of his company was delayed until 1935, due to the Great Depression.

When it opened, it was where celebrities went to get their hair and makeup done, in state-of-the-art factories encompassing four floors. The second floor was for wigs and hair, the third floor was where Max Factor invented tube lipstick, and on the fourth floor he worked with powder products, eye shadow, face powder and rouge.

Separate makeup rooms were customized for redheads, brunettes, blondes, and brownettes. It's where Lucille Ball (born with

Housed inside the historic Max Factor building, The Hollywood Museum's ground floor is dedicated to Max Factor, Hollywood's makeup king. Photo courtesy of The Hollywood Museum

Max Factor had designated makeup rooms for blondes, brunettes, brownettes, and redheads (shown here).

brown hair) became a redhead, Jean Harlow a blonde, and Judy Garland got her pigtails for Dorothy in the *Wizard of Oz*.

The crown jewel was the elegant art deco lobby, designed with 22-karat gold and silver leafing, white and rose-colored marble, chandeliers, trompe l'oeil, and antique furniture.

"This lobby plays a very important role. It was not only to greet celebrities, but to make it okay for women to buy makeup," said Donelle Dadigan, who purchased the building in 1996 from Procter & Gamble. The building had changed ownership several times after Max Factor's son, Max Factor Jr., sold it in 1973. (Max Factor's great-grandsons launched Smashbox Cosmetics in 1996, and Max Factor makeup was discontinued in the US in 2006.)

It took nine years to restore the Max Factor building to its original 1930s grandeur. The ground floor houses the historic dressing rooms (complete with furniture, makeup, brushes, etc.) and many original displays from the old Max Factor Studio.

Located inside the historic Max Factor Building, The Hollywood Museum (which debuted in 2003) houses over 10,000 pieces of authentic Hollywood memorabilia, including costumes, props, photographs, scripts, stars' car collections and personal artifacts, and posters from popular films and TV shows. The lower level, which contained a bowling alley and speakeasy during Prohibition and Max Factor's tenure, features a jail cell corridor and props from the film Silence of the Lambs.

OLDEST HOT DOG STAND
PINK'S HOT DOGS
709 N La Brea Ave.

When Paul and Betty Pink started Pink's Hot Dogs in 1939, a hot dog sold for 10 cents and cokes were a nickel. Pink's offered curb service and sold about 100 hot dogs a day.

Today, the iconic Hollywood landmark sells about 2,000 hot dogs and 200 hamburgers a day. The hot dog stand itself, although expanded a weeny bit, hasn't changed much since its humble beginnings and remains in the original location at La Brea and Melrose avenues, on a designated "Pink's Corner."

Paul and Betty Pink bought a pushcart for $50 with money borrowed from Betty's mother. With no on-site electricity, they used a 100-yard extension cord to fire up the cart for the first two years. It was plugged into a friendly neighbor's outlet.

They paid $15 a month to lease the land to house the pushcart. In 1941, when the landlord raised their rent from $15 to $25 per month, the Pinks obtained a bank loan for $4,000 and purchased the land. They added a cover to the pushcart, enabling them to grill hamburgers. The menu was basic: A chili dog and a hamburger. The price of the hot dog in 1946 was 25 cents.

Next, the Pinks added on to the small hot dog stand, which is the current building. Their son, Richard Pink, began working at Pink's in 1960

Pink's is so popular with celebrities that many of the unique hog dogs are named after them. Photo courtesy of Pink's Hot Dogs

The Martha Stewart dog, which she created herself, is topped with relish, onions, bacon, chopped tomatoes, sauerkraut, and sour cream. Photo courtesy of Pink's Hot Dogs

at age 16. "My favorite job was making hot dogs for customers and chatting with them after I served them," said Pink, who later earned a law degree.

When Paul and Betty retired in 1985, Richard, his wife, Gloria, and his sister, Beverly, took over the operation of Pink's. Since then, the family has created over 40 combinations of hot dogs and 12 varieties of hamburgers. With Pink's proximity to major Hollywood studios, it began attracting movie and TV stars.

Many of the hot dogs are named after stars. The most popular franks are The Brando (mustard, onions, chili, and cheddar cheese), and The Martha Stewart (relish, onions, bacon, chopped tomatoes, sauerkraut, and sour cream), created by the celebrity herself. In addition to attracting stars, Pink's has been in many movies and TV shows.

According to Richard Pink, as the Pink's name grew, large restaurant operators approached the family to license the Pink's name and products in various shopping malls, amusement parks, hotels, arenas, and county fairs. Pink's now has 13 locations, including Los Angeles County, Orange County, Ventura County, New York, Wisconsin, Hawaii and the Philippines.

WEST L.A.

—1862

OLDEST
JEWISH CONGREGATION
WILSHIRE BOULEVARD TEMPLE
3663 Wilshire Blvd.

The landmark Wilshire Boulevard Temple is not only home to the oldest Jewish congregation (and largest, with 4,500 members) in Los Angeles, it's also recognized for its majestic architectural design.

From 1862 to 1933 it was known as Congregation B'nai B'rith. It received its charter in 1862, when Abraham Lincoln was president. Rabbi Joseph Newmark organized Congregation B'nai B'rith as an Orthodox temple in 1862, making it the first synagogue in Los Angeles. The congregation met in various locations until Wilshire Boulevard Temple was built in 1929.

Designed by architect Abram M. Edelman, the temple is a hybrid of Byzantine and Romanesque styles and boasts a striking, domed synagogue. It was built with the support of temple members who were the city's leading land developers, bankers, politicians, merchants, and movie studio moguls, including the Warner brothers, Carl Laemmle, Irving Thalberg, Sol Lesser, and Louis B. Mayer.

The temple's crown jewel is the Magnin Sanctuary, named after Rabbi Edgar F. Magnin, who served the congregation for nearly 70 years. Murals surrounding the interior tell the story of the Jews, from Abraham through discovery of the New

Wilshire Boulevard Temple offers tours of its architectural design.
Photo courtesy of Wilshire Boulevard Temple

World. The murals were commissioned by the Warner brothers and executed by artist and silent film director Hugo Ballin.

Wilshire Boulevard Temple is a City of Los Angeles Historic Cultural Monument and is listed on the National Register of Historic Places.

Wilshire Boulevard Temple has three campuses: the original temple in Koreatown, another facility on the west side called Irmas Campus that was built in more recent years, and the third campus in Brentwood, called University Campus, that recently joined with the congregation. Tours are available of the temple architecture, the donors, and the progression of the temple.

OLDEST CANALS
VENICE CANALS
Located off 25th St. in Venice Beach

T he scenic Venice Canals, built in 1905 by developer Abbot Kinney, are in a secluded residential neighborhood a few blocks from Venice Beach. Only six canals remain from the elaborate network created by Kinney as part of his Venice of America plan to recreate the appearance and ambiance of Venice, Italy, in Southern California.

First mules, and then steam shovels, were used to excavate the saltwater marshland. But by the 1920s cars were quickly gaining popularity, and the canals were viewed as outdated. Consequently, many of the canals were filled in to make paved

Tucked in a Venice Beach neighborhood, the Venice Canals were designed to resemble Venice, Italy.

roads. By 1940, the remaining canals had fallen into disrepair, and the sidewalks were condemned by the city.

The entire Venice district remained in poor condition for more than 40 years, and proposals to renovate the canals were unsuccessful due to lack of funding, environmental concerns, and disputes over who should bear the financial responsibility.

The canals were renovated in 1992; they were drained, and new sidewalks and walls were built. The canals reopened in 1993, and multimillion-dollar homes flank the six canals. Many homes have private docks for non-motorized watercraft.

The public is welcome to walk along the sidewalks and bridges spanning the canals. The residential district surrounding the remaining canals was listed on the National Register of Historic Places in 1982.

The Venice Beach Boardwalk was built in 1905, also as part of Abbot Kinney's Venice of America plan. The funky, two-mile Ocean Front Walk features a variety of street entertainers, as well as cafes and shops.

Oldest Seaside Attractions

Santa Monica Pier

200 Santa Monica Pier, Santa Monica

When the whimsical, beachside Looff Hippodrome was built in 1916, its style defined the Southern California beach culture in the early 1900s. The Moorish/Byzantine/California-style structure, designed with a circular roof over a carousel, was the last work of famous carousel manufacturer Charles I.D. Looff. The hippodrome was declared a National Historic Landmark in 1987.

Also in 1916, Looff built the Looff Pleasure Pier for amusement park thrill rides, including the Blue Streak Racer roller coaster. He installed his pier next to the Santa Monica Pier, which was built in 1909 as a conduit for the city's sewage. The side-by-side piers look like one pier, known as the Santa Monica Pier.

Over the years, pier attractions changed often. The Blue Streak Racer was torn down and replaced with the faster Whirlwind Dipper in 1924. The original merry-go-round was replaced in 1947 with a 1922 Philadelphia Toboggan Company carousel with 44 hand-carved and hand-painted wooden horses, which were restored in 1990. Various amusement rides came and went, from the 1950s to the early 1990s. Arcades and gift shops were added. In 1983, annual concerts known as the Twilight Dance Series joined the lively pier.

In 1996, Pacific Park opened as the first year-round amusement park on the pier since the 1930s. The amusement park features 12 thrilling rides, including the West Coaster, and Pacific Wheel—the world's first solar-powered Ferris wheel. The nine-story Ferris wheel lifts riders more than 130 feet above the ocean.

Top: *Named after the ancient Greek hippodrome stadiums used for horse and chariot racing, the Looff Hippodrome houses a carousel on the main floor and city offices on the second. Photo courtesy of the Santa Monica Pier Corporation*

Tucked beneath the pier is the Heal the Bay Aquarium, featuring over 100 species of local

Bottom: *The carousel features 44 antique hand-carved wooden horses and two sleighs (one modified for ADA compliance) lit up by 1,100 electric lights. A Wurlitzer band organ plays music.*

marine life, hands-on activities, and educational programs.

Today, more than four million people visit the pier annually to enjoy the amusement park, restaurants, shops, and the carousel inside the hippodrome.

At the base of the pier, Big Dean's Ocean Front Cafe is a casual beach eatery where customers can enjoy pub food, drinks, and ocean views. When it opened in 1902 it was called Laring's Lunch Room. Big Dean's took over in the 1970s. 1615 Ocean Front Walk.

——————————1918

OLDEST PRIVATE ART COLLEGE
OTIS COLLEGE OF ART AND DESIGN
9045 Lincoln Blvd.

From Oscar awardees, legendary costume designers, and leaders of contemporary art movements to design stars at Apple, DreamWorks, and Disney (among other high-profile companies), Otis alumni include A-list professionals in their respective fields who have graduated from the prestigious art college.

Named after *Los Angeles Times* founder Harrison Gray Otis, the Otis College of Art and Design was the city's first independent professional school of art. It remains a major art institution in California, offering degrees in a wide variety of visual and applied arts, media, and design.

Otis' main campus is located in a landmark Mid-Century Modern-style building. Photo courtesy of Otis College of Art and Design

Otis College of Art and Design has separate campuses that specialize in various art programs. Photo courtesy of Fawad Assadullah/Otis College of Art and Design

Originally named the Otis Art Institute (the name changed several times over the decades), it was established in 1918 when Otis donated his home—known as Bivouac—to L.A. County to be used for the advancement of the arts.

Throughout the 1940s, Normal Rockwell spent his winters as an artist-in-residence, painting many of his famed *Saturday Evening Post* covers, and using Otis students as his models.

A ceramics school was begun by Peter Voulkos in the 1950s and was part of arts movements such as the Craft-to-Art movement. In 1991, the name changed from Otis School of Art and Design to Otis College of Art and Design. Six years later, Otis relocated its main campus to its current location in Westchester.

In 1997, the main campus moved into the former IBM Aerospace headquarters in Westchester. Designed by architect Eliot Noyes, the vintage-1964 IBM building is famous for its computer punch card-style windows.

OLDEST AIRPORT
LOS ANGELES INTERNATIONAL AIRPORT (LAX)
1 World Way

In 1928, wheat, barley, and lima bean fields were converted into landing strips for the newly formed Department of Airports. A 2,000-foot, oiled landing strip and two 100-foot hangars, each with a 20-plane capacity, were built on the south side of the airport.

The official dedication of the airport, then known as Mines Field, took place on June 7, 1930. The City of Los Angeles bought the airport in 1937. The name became Los Angeles Airport in 1941 and was renamed Los Angeles International Airport (LAX) in 1949. LAX has four runways that each run in an east-west configuration. In 1946, most airline companies moved their fights and facilities there from the San Fernando Valley's Lockheed field,

Left: *Actress Viola Peter at the dedication ceremony for the Los Angeles Municipal Airport June 7, 1930.*

Right: *The landmark Theme Building was a restaurant for several years.*

Photos courtesy of Los Angeles World Airports

Cathay Airlines is the flag carrier for Hong Kong. Photo courtesy of Los Angeles World Airports

which had been the region's major airport.

Many of LAX's modern improvements date from the 1950s and 1960s. These include a new air traffic control tower, and the landmark Theme Building, a saucer-shaped restaurant (currently vacant) with 135-foot-high parabolic arches. Designed by architect William Pereira as a symbol of the "first airport of the jet age," it was completed in 1961. That same year, the Central Terminal Area opened, 15 years after commercial service began at the airport.

After additional improvements beginning in the 1970s and continuing today, LAX has state-of-the-art terminals, hangars, and service facilities.

In the 1930s, the main airports were the Hollywood Burbank Airport (then known as Union Air Terminal, and later Lockheed, and the Bob Hope Airport) in Burbank and the Grand Central Airport in Glendale (which closed in 1959). The Hollywood Burbank Airport, which has two terminals, is a favorite with locals for its easy in-and-out service.

—1931

OLDEST PUBLIC WATER FOUNTAIN
ELECTRIC FOUNTAIN
9439 Santa Monica Blvd., Beverly Hills

With its rainbow-colored water and elaborate art sculptures, it's no wonder the Electric Fountain has been attracting motorists and pedestrians since its installation in Beverly Gardens Park in Beverly Hills in 1931. The first public fountain in the country, it was designed by architect Ralph Carlin Flewelling. The sculpture atop the fountain was designed by Robert Merrell Gage. The historic fountain commands a prominent position in Beverly Gardens Park, a 1.9-mile linear park that spans 23 blocks on Santa Monica Boulevard from Wilshire Boulevard to Doheny Drive.

The fountain—which cost $22,000 to build—was given to Beverly Hills by the mother of silent-screen star Harold Lloyd. A celebrity in her own right, Sarah Lloyd was a visionary and pioneer of Beverly Hills. The fountain's installation was paid for by the Women's Club of Beverly Hills, over which she presided for a time.

The fountain's focal point is the six-foot granite sculpture of a Tongva Native American tribe member, kneeling in prayer, on a 20-foot stone column. The sculpture is symbolic of an Indian rain prayer and pays homage to the area's early inhabitants.

The sculpture is surrounded by bas relief stone sculptures on

The Electric Fountain is a water fountain with public art sculptures and evening lighting. Photo courtesy of the City of Beverly Hills

a three-foot-high, circular fountain wall depicting scenes from the area's early history and development. The Mosaic terra-cotta tile pavement insets illustrate the community's early history. The color lighting program is at dusk. The fountain and statue were restored by California Waters in 2016.

Greystone Mansion and Gardens: The Doheny Estate is a Beverly Hills historic landmark. Construction on the stone mansion began in 1927 and took over three years to complete, at a cost of over $3 million. Five months after homeowner Ned Doheny, his wife, and their five children moved in, he was found shot to death in an apparent murder-suicide by a friend and aide. The mansion's ownership changed hands a few times, until the City of Beverly Hills purchased the hilltop property in 1965 for about $1.3 million to install a 19-million-gallon water tank to serve as the city's reservoir. In 1971, the entire site, including the mansion, was dedicated as a public park. 905 Loma Vista Dr.

SOUTH BAY

OLDEST EXISTING NEWSPAPER

LOS ANGELES TIMES
2300 E Imperial Hwy., El Segundo

The *Los Angeles Times* (known as the *Times*) is a daily newspaper with a circulation of 653,868 on weekdays and 954,010 on Sundays. It has the fifth-largest circulation in the US, and has won over 40 Pulitzer Prizes.

Founded by Nathan Cole, Jr. and Thomas Gardiner, the newspaper was originally called the *Los Angeles Daily Times* and was first published on December 4, 1881. The newspaper became the *Los Angeles Times* when the word "Daily" was removed from the name in October 1886. The newspaper's first home was a small brick building at Temple and New High streets in downtown Los Angeles.

About a year after Cole and Gardiner launched the newspaper, they couldn't pay the printing bill and it was inherited by its printer, the Mirror Printing Office and Book Bindery. Former military officer

The Los Angeles Times *was located in an Art Deco building from 1935 until its move to El Segundo in 2018.*

Harrison Gray Otis was hired as editor and transformed the paper into a financial success.

Otis and a partner purchased the *Times* and Mirror properties in 1884 and incorporated them as the Times-Mirror Company. Two years later, Otis purchased his partner's interest in the company. When Otis died in 1917, his son-in-law Harry Chandler became the second publisher, starting a tradition of Chandler family ownership of the *Times* until they sold it in 2000 to the Tribune Media Company.

In 1935, the newspaper moved to a new, landmark art deco building, eventually taking up an entire city block that became known as Times Mirror Square.

As the newspaper grew, it developed from a regional daily into one of the world's great newspapers. Over time, as the staff expanded and new *Times* bureaus opened in the US and abroad, the *Times* shifted its focus from conservative to balanced journalism.

The struggling newspaper industry and financial challenges prompted a series of changes in ownership and editors-in-chief. In January 2018, the paper's staff voted to unionize. Shortly after the *Los Angeles Times* was sold for $500 million to local biotech billionaire Patrick Soon-Shiong, he moved the headquarters to El Segundo.

A cultural landmark, Old Town Music Hall is a 1921 El Segundo State Theater that houses a 1925 Mighty Wurlitzer Theater Pipe Organ. The theater shows silent films that are accompanied by the wind-powered pipe organ. 140 Richmond St.

─────────────────────────1903

OLDEST BOAT SHOP
THE AL LARSON BOAT SHOP (ALBS)
1046 S Seaside Ave., San Pedro

Five years before Los Angeles had a port, Swedish immigrant Al Larson established the Al Larson Boat Shop in East San Pedro in 1903. Lacking electricity at that time, the shop performed all the repairs and new construction without any power tools. The shop initially built and repaired wooden fishing vessels for local fishermen.

But shipbuilding soon developed into a major industry with the development of the Port of Los Angeles on December 9, 1907. With lucrative contracts from the US Navy and the booming fishing industry at Fish Harbor, Al Larson relocated his shop from the Wilmington waterfront to nearby Fish Harbor in 1924.

During World War II, the boat shop built YMS-1 Class auxiliary motor minesweepers for the US Navy. Operations slowed after the war ended and shipbuilding declined. Since 1959, the business has been owned and operated by Andrew Wall and his family, which has a long boating history dating to 15th-century Venice.

By the 1960s, Wall had improved the shop, adding two nearby buildings, a new marina, and a new dry dock to service yachts, fishing boats, and small, government-owned boats. Today, the shop consists of 7.70 acres: 2.35 acres of land and 5.35 acres of water, including docks, piers, and a marina.

The boat shop is the last shipyard in the Port of Los Angeles, and the oldest marine repair facility in Southern California.

The Al Larson Boat Shop is the last shipyard in the Port of Los Angeles, and the oldest marine repair facility in Southern California. Photo courtesy of Al Larson Boat Shop

The commercial yard handles vessels from 50 feet to 265 feet, but few private boats. Typically, it maintains and repairs tugboats, government vessels, barges, offshore oil equipment, ferries, fireboats, working boats, research vessels, and yachts, as well as other types of marine equipment.

Over the years, the boat shop has worked on many interesting boats, including the *Wild Goose* (John Wayne's), now owned by Hornblower Cruises, target ships from Naval Air, fireboats from Port of Long Beach, and Lindblad's National Geographic vessels.

Not surprisingly, the boatyard is a popular film location. Movies include *Face/Off* with John Travolta and Nicholas Cage, *Pearl Harbor* with Ben Affleck, and *Charlie's Angels* with Drew Barrymore. Studio productions include CBS' *NCIS*, and Columbia Pictures' *Spiderman IV*.

Located in San Pedro Bay, the Port of Los Angeles (the busiest container port in North America) features passenger, cruise, and cargo terminals, and the 400-acre L.A. Waterfront is home to historic sites, coastal promenades, seaside dining, special events, and museums, including the L.A. Maritime Museum.

OLDEST OPERATING LIGHTHOUSE
LOS ANGELES HARBOR LIGHTHOUSE (ANGEL'S GATE LIGHT)
Los Angeles Harbor, San Pedro

P rofessional mariners and recreational boaters have been welcomed to the Los Angeles Harbor by the distinctive green flash of the Los Angeles Harbor Lighthouse (better known as Angel's Gate Light) since 1913. And the two-note blast of its foghorn every 30 seconds is a familiar sound to local residents.

Designed differently from other California lighthouses, the Los Angeles Harbor Lighthouse is situated on a 40-foot concrete square at the San Pedro Breakwater in Los Angeles Harbor.

In order to withstand severe stormy weather, the lighthouse was built with a structural steel framework and steel plates. The breakwater is 9,250 feet long and contains nearly three million tons of rock, brought over from Santa Catalina Island.

In 1939, the sturdy lighthouse survived a violent, five-day storm that caused the 73-foot Romanesque tower to lean slightly toward shore. But it stands to this day.

When the lighthouse was automated in 1973, it eliminated the need for keepers.

Later, in the 1980s, the Coast Guard converted the lighthouse to solar power, and the original Fresnel lens was loaned to the Los Angeles Maritime Museum.

Although the lighthouse is not open for walking tours, boat tours give passengers a close-up view. Photo courtesy of the Port of Los Angeles

When a ship enters the Los Angeles Harbor on a maiden voyage, the City of L.A. presents the captain with a plaque etched with the likeness of the lighthouse. The plaque represents an official greeting from the city.

The lighthouse celebrated its 100th birthday after an extensive renovation on October 27, 2013. Although the lighthouse is not open for walking tours, harbor boat tours offer close-up views.

Although no longer operational, the Point Fermin Lighthouse was the first navigational light in the San Pedro Bay. The ornate Victorian structure was built with lumber from California redwoods and completed in 1874. It remained in operation until 1941. Due to the bombing of Pearl Harbor there was increased concern that its light would act as a beacon for enemy planes or ships. The lighthouse opened for free public tours in 2003. 807 W Paseo Del Mar, San Pedro.

OLDEST AQUARIUM
CABRILLO MARINE AQUARIUM
3720 Stephen M. White Dr., San Pedro

O riginally called the Cabrillo Marine Museum, the aquarium had humble beginnings as a collection of specimens housed in the Cabrillo Beach Bathhouse in 1935. Lifeguard John Olguin persuaded a colleague to transfer his growing collection of marine specimens from Venice Beach to the Cabrillo Beach Bathhouse in San Pedro.

By 1937, the museum collection grew to more than 100,000 specimens, establishing Cabrillo as the only full-size marine museum in Los Angeles County. After Olguin was appointed director of the museum, he began giving talks to visiting school groups, and later field trips. The field trips were so popular that he recruited volunteers to assist with tours and beach walks.

In 1951, under Olguin's leadership, the museum began an evening program that highlighted a local marine phenomenon— grunion fish spawning on the beach. This unique and popular program continues to this day.

As the museum's collections and visitors grew, it required a larger facility. On October 21, 1981, the new, $3 million Frank Gehry-designed Cabrillo Marine Museum held its grand opening.

In 1993, the museum changed its name to Cabrillo Marine Aquarium (CMA) to highlight its living collections and to prepare for future expansion.

The Cabrillo Marine Aquarium, an educational and research facility, features touch tanks, an aquatic nursery and exhibits about local marine life. Photos courtesy of the Cabrillo Marine Aquarium

Today, the Cabrillo Marine Aquarium is an educational and research facility with numerous aquariums, touch tanks, an aquatic nursery, and exhibits about local marine life. CMA is considered a top educational public aquarium and a trusted resource that inspires exploration, respect, and conservation of Southern California marine life.

The aquarium's original home, the 1932 Cabrillo Beach Bathhouse, was renovated and serves as a recreational facility. 3800 Stephen M White Dr. Nearby historic sites include Angel's Gate Park, composed of the Point Fermin Lighthouse, Korean Friendship Bell (presented to the US by the South Korean government in 1975 to commemorate the United States bicentennial and as a token of friendship), and the Fort MacArthur Museum (a former US Army post that guarded the Los Angeles Harbor from 1914 to 1974). 3601 S Gaffey St.

San Gabriel Valley/ Crescenta Valley

OLDEST MISSION
SAN GABRIEL MISSION
428 S Mission Dr., San Gabriel

Founded on September 8, 1771 by Franciscan Father Junipero Serra, the San Gabriel Mission is the fourth of California's 21 missions.

Built of stone, brick, and mortar, it's among the best-preserved of all the missions. The altar was handcrafted in Mexico City and brought to the mission in the 1790s. The six polychrome wooden statues were hand-carved in Spain.

At its peak in 1829, the mission had 50,000 livestock, 160,000 grapevines, and 2,300 fruit trees. For years, the mission was the valley's spiritual center. The last Franciscan left in 1852, and in 1855 the US Land Commission awarded the property to the diocese of Mission San Gabriel Arcangel. The Claretian priests have overseen the mission's care since 1908. The mission continues to serve as the cornerstone for the Catholic faith community in Los Angeles County.

But the mission's legacy is complicated. While it's considered by historians to be an essential link to California's past, the mission's friars also forced indigenous people into labor and coerced them into converting to Catholicism and assimilating to their culture. Thousands of unnamed indigenous people are buried below what is now a small Catholic cemetery.

On July 11, 2020, a fire set by an arsonist destroyed the roof, most of the refurbished pews and portions of the interior,

SAN GABRIEL VALLEY/CRESCENTA VALLEY **121**

The San Gabriel Mission is the fourth of California's 21 missions. Photo courtesy of Nataly Hernandez

though some statues, historic items, and artifacts survived. At the time, the mission was undergoing renovation for its 250th anniversary. The mission is expected to reopen in 2022.

Franciscan Father Junipero Serra has long been considered one of California's founding fathers and was made a saint by the Catholic Church in 2015. This outraged many activists, who blame the mission system for enslaving and killing indigenous people. The San Gabriel Mission moved its statue of Serra into its garden, out of public view.

OLDEST GRAPEVINE
SAN GABRIEL MISSION
428 S Mission Dr., San Gabriel

It may come as a surprise, even to some locals, but in the 19th century Los Angeles was a major wine producer. In fact, DNA testing performed by UC Davis in 2014 traced a direct descendant of plantings made by Father Junipero Serra in the 1770s at San Gabriel Mission.

That was exciting news for the L.A. Vintners Association, which had been asked by the mission to help propagate some vines. "We took a look around and saw grapes!" said Mark Blatty, a vintner member and proprietor of Byron Blatty Wines. "I had been to the mission as a kid and remembered there being old vines there."

According to the DNA test, the plantings were a cross between Vitis girdiana—a wild grape in Southern California—and Vitis vinifera, also known as a mission grape, a prolific varietal that was carried from Spain and planted across the Americas. The mission's oldest vine is known as the Mother Vine or Trinity Vine.

The planting of vineyards by Franciscan friars at California missions was common, since grapes were needed for sacramental wine to perform the rite of communion.

By the 1830s, the vineyards at San Gabriel expanded to more than 170 acres, producing as much as 50,000 gallons of wine per year. The cuttings from the original San Gabriel vine were also planted in today's downtown L.A. Grapevines can be seen creeping through trellises at Avila Adobe, L.A.'s first residence., in

The oldest vines still producing grapes were planted in the 1770s at the San Gabriel Mission. Photo courtesy of Terri Huerta

El Pueblo de Los Angeles Historical Monument.

The flourishing vines provided the foundation for the Southern California's wine industry—that is, until the arrival of European immigrants who brought French varieties, such as Cabernet Franc and Sauvignon Blanc. In comparison, the mission grape was considered inferior, producing a dull table wine.

But it was the spread of Pierce's disease, an insect-transmitted bacteria in the 1880s, that wiped out the thousands of acres of vineyards, essentially crushing the wine business as farmers turned to more profitable orange and walnut production.

In the meantime, the original vines at San Gabriel Mission continued to thrive, apparently fed by an underground aquifer. The four most robust vines form a dense overgrowth spanning hundreds of square feet of the mission grounds. The roots of the largest, the Ramona vine planted in 1861, are as thick as a tree trunk.

Members of the L.A. Vintners Association recently took cuttings and grapes from the mission vines to make wine and replant in other vineyards. The plan is to use the grapes (that have a sweet flavor and bitter tannins) to produce a wine known as Angelica, a semisweet wine similar to Port, and the kind of wine produced by Franciscans. The vintners made a barrel of Angelica for the mission's 250th anniversary.

OLDEST ANNUAL PARADE
TOURNAMENT OF ROSES PARADE
Colorado Blvd., Pasadena

The annual Tournament of Roses Parade is practically synonymous with New Year's Day. Rain or shine, the two-hour parade starts at 8 a.m. (PST) and features elaborate floral floats, marching bands, and high-stepping equestrian units along the 5 ½ mile route along Colorado Boulevard.

Each parade features a Grand Marshal. In the past, these included Shirley Temple (1939, 1989, 1999), Mary Pickford (1933), Bob Hope (1947, 1969), and Walt Disney (1966). The themed parades also feature a Rose Queen and Royal Court.

The weather is usually perfect, although there have been 10 rainy days. The annual procession was canceled in 2021 due to COVID-19 concerns, marking only the fourth cancelation in the parade's history. The 2022 parade, themed "Dream.Believe. Achieve.," took place under sunny skies.

The first parade was in 1890 when Pasadena's Valley Hunt Club, led by Professor Charles Frederick Holder, invited its former East Coast neighbors to a midwinter holiday to watch games, including chariot races, jousting, foot races, polo, and tug-of-war on the town lot (renamed Tournament Park in 1900) under the warm California sun.

The abundance of fresh flowers prompted the club to add a parade before the competition and name it Tournament of Roses. Entrants decorated their carriages with hundreds of colorful

blooms. In the following years, the festival expanded to include marching bands and motorized floats. Reviewing stands were built along the parade route. When the festival grew too large for the Valley Hunt Club to handle, the Tournament of Roses Association was formed in 1895.

The annual Tournament of Roses Parade features elaborately decorated floral floats, bands, and equestrian units. Photo courtesy of the Tournament of Roses Parade Collection, Glendale History Room, Glendale Library, Arts & Culture

Initially, entrants made their own floats. In 1913, Isabelle Coleman, who had the first professional float-building company, built a float for the local Realty Board. By 1916 she was commissioned to do three floats in the Rose Parade. Although a few floats are still built by volunteers from their sponsoring communities, most are built by professional float-building companies and take nearly a year to construct. Fiesta Parade Floats, which has been with the Tournament the longest, started in 1988. Currently, the only cities that build their own floats are Downey, South Pasadena, Burbank, Cal Poly, La Canada, and Sierra Madre.

Today's floats feature high-tech computerized animation and natural materials. More than 80,000 hours of combined manpower is supplied by 935 volunteer members of the Tournament of Roses Association.

On parade day, thousands of spectators line up early, many even camping out the night before to secure prime viewing spots, while millions around the world admire the parade on TV. After the parade, the Rose Parade Showcase features a two-mile display of Rose Parade floats on January 1 and 2.

Oldest Independent Bookstore
Vroman's Bookstore

695 E Colorado Blvd., Pasadena
3729 E Foothill Blvd., Pasadena

Since its founding in 1894, Vroman's Bookstore has stayed relevant, evolving with the times and establishing itself as a Pasadena institution, literary landmark, and gathering place for customers browsing for books and gifts. It's not only the oldest independent, family-owned bookstore in the L.A. area, but also in Southern California.

"Vroman's longevity is a testament to people, including the customers and community who have supported and partnered with us and the employees who have contributed their time and energy to make Vroman's a special place," said Julia Cowlishaw, Vroman's chief executive officer.

Vroman's was founded by Adam Clark Vroman, who moved to Pasadena in the late 1800s, hoping the weather would improve his wife, Esther's, health. She died two years later and Vroman sold his book collection to raise the capital to open a bookstore. He was a photographer and philanthropist who supported the Pasadena Public Library.

When he died in 1916, he left the bookstore to several employees, including Allan David Sheldon, whose descendants have been owners for decades. Sheldon's great nephew, Joel

Vroman Sheldon III, is the current chairman of the company.

Throughout the years, Vroman's has gained a reputation for its free community events, children's storytimes, craft classes, and world-class author signings. The store has hosted authors who include President Bill Clinton, President Jimmy Carter, Barbara Walters, Ray Bradbury, and many others.

A Pasadena institution, Vroman's Bookstore has an extensive book inventory as well as gifts. Outside, there's a blast from the past—an authentic newsstand. Top photo courtesy of Vroman's Bookstore

The store is also known for its extensive book inventory, array of gifts, in-house coffee shop, and outdoor newsstand. In 2008, Vroman's was honored with the Publishers Weekly Bookseller of the Year award. The following year, Vroman's bought the West Hollywood bookstore, the Book Soup, after its owner died. The Vroman's Gives Back charitable program donates a portion of customers' purchases to local nonprofits and programs.

Vroman's latest addition is the 1894 wine and beer bar, located in its bookstore on Colorado Blvd. Named after the year Vroman's opened, the 1894 features literature-inspired cocktails, craft beer, wine flights, and small bites.

OLDEST BOTANICAL GARDENS

THE HUNTINGTON LIBRARY, ART MUSEUM & BOTANICAL GARDENS

1151 Oxford Rd., San Marino

A mong L.A.'s best local getaways is The Huntington Library, Art Museum & Botanical Gardens. Nestled in a serene residential neighborhood, The Huntington provides Angelenos and visitors a place to slow down and smell the roses and other floral beauties in 16 themed gardens spanning 120 acres. The gardens include a Rose Garden, Japanese Garden, Desert Garden, Children's Garden, Jungle Garden, and Shakespeare Garden. Cozy paths with benches meander through the gardens, over bridges, and around lily ponds.

The Huntington started as the private gardens of Southern California's largest landowner (and developer of the Pacific Electric Railway Company), Henry E. Huntington, and evolved into a cultural institution piece by piece, or rather, garden by garden. In 1903, Huntington bought the San Marino Ranch, a working ranch about 12 miles from downtown L.A. with citrus groves, nut and fruit orchards, alfalfa crops, a small herd of cows, and poultry.

He and his wife, Arabella, lived in a mansion he built to house his collection of paintings, books, and manuscripts, and hired William Hertrich to develop the gardens. Hertrich first established

The lily ponds were among the first to be developed at The Huntington Library, Art Museum & Botanical Gardens, at the time the private estate of Henry E. Huntington. Photos courtesy of The Huntington Library, Art Museum & Botanical Gardens

a nursery, which soon grew to over 15,000 plants. Since pepper trees were one of Huntington's favorites, Hertrich made sure to plant many of those. The lily ponds were next, in 1904, followed by the palm and cactus gardens. The Huntington's famous Rose Garden was originally created in 1908 for the private enjoyment of Henry and Arabella Huntington (roses were her favorite).

The development of the estate was ongoing and evolved into 120 acres of diverse botanical collections surrounding two art galleries and a library showcasing collections of rare books and manuscripts, European art from the 15th to the early 20th century, and American art from the late 17th to the mid-20th century.

In 1919, Henry and Arabella Huntington signed the trust document that established The Huntington as a public, collections-based, research and educational institution. The Huntington opened to the public in 1928.

As part of The Huntington's centennial celebration (of the signing of the trust document in 1919), a yellow and orchid pink floribunda was hybridized by Tom Carruth, The Huntington's E. L. and Ruth B. Shannon Curator of the Rose Collections. The "Huntington's 100th" variety of rose can be seen in the Rose Garden and in other spots on the property. It's also available for purchase.

OLDEST OBSERVATORY
MOUNT WILSON OBSERVATORY
Mt. Wilson peak, San Gabriel Mountains

From its perch at 5,700-feet elevation in the Angeles National Forest, the Mount Wilson Observatory offers astronomical views of the universe, as well as of cities, valleys and the Pacific Ocean. But the star attractions are the observatory's

The Mount Wilson Observatory is comprised of a group of telescopes and a museum.

towers and telescopes.

The observatory was founded in 1904 by the newly established Carnegie Institution of Washington (DC) under the leadership of George Ellery Hale. He had previously founded the Yerkes Observatory in Wisconsin.

An astrophysics pioneer, Hale was especially interested in the sun, since it is the closest star and the easiest to study. He placed such importance on studying the sun that the site was known as the Mount Wilson Solar Observatory until 1919.

The observatory grounds consist of 60- to 150-foot-high solar telescopes, 60- and 100-inch telescopes, the Berkeley Infrared Spatial Interferometer, the Center for High Angular Resolution Astronomy (CHARA) Array, an exhibit hall, and a small astronomical museum displaying historical photographs, letters, and a scale model of the observatory.

The observatory is credited with the discoveries of galaxies outside the Milky Way, and the expanding universe—the "Big Bang" theory. In the 1920s, American astronomer Edwin Hubble used photographic plates from the observatory's 100-inch telescope to confirm that the Andromeda Galaxy was a separate galaxy beyond the Milky Way.

Also on observatory grounds is the Cosmic Cafe, a casual eatery with outdoor tables. A US Forest Service Adventure Pass is required to park at the observatory. It's $5 for a day pass, $30 for an annual pass, available at sporting goods stores, ranger stations, and other places.

Since the Angeles Crest Highway (the route to the observatory) wasn't built until 1935, all the components for the original telescopes were hauled nine miles from the valley floor up a narrow dirt road, initially by mule-drawn wagons. Today, Angeles Crest Highway provides a scenic drive through the forest, which has trails and picnic areas.

OLDEST PHARMACY
FAIR OAKS PHARMACY & SODA FOUNTAIN
1526 Mission St., South Pasadena

Although the pharmacy's name and owners changed over the years, it's in the original location and looks much like it did as a corner drugstore, where people would grab a bite to eat while waiting for their prescriptions. Its location along a part of Route 66 made the pharmacy a popular rest stop. The building was originally owned and financed by Gertrude Ozmun,

Fair Oaks Pharmacy & Soda Fountain is an old-fashioned corner pharmacy that carries a little bit of everything.

an "entrepreneur of her time," who paid $14,000 for the corner lot in 1914.

It was first called the South Pasadena Pharmacy, then the Raymond Pharmacy in the '20s and '30s, and finally Fair Oaks Pharmacy and Soda Fountain in the 1940s. The one-stop shop is decked out with retro-red stools, neon lights and vintage Coca-Cola signage. In the 1990s, the pharmacy was restored to its original design with authentic tin ceilings, honeycomb tile floors, and antique pharmacy fixtures.

In the early days, pharmacists sold phosphate sodas and ice cream while working the lunch counter and filling prescriptions for the day. Now, soda jerks serve lunch and scoop ice cream at the old-fashioned soda fountain counter, featuring over 100 items on the menu, including sandwiches, burgers, hot dogs, salads, and breakfast options. Ice cream includes generous-sized banana splits, shakes, sundaes, ice cream sodas, phosphates, and egg creams.

And like the early pharmacists—who crafted their own medicinal recipes—current owner and pharmacist Zahra Shahniani practices compounding. She specializes in creating custom remedies to match anyone's medical demands, from children who are picky toward certain flavors to animals who require important medical attention.

In addition to the pharmacy and soda fountain counter, Fair Oaks' shelves are stuffed with vintage games and toys, old-fashioned candy, Christmas ornaments, Marilyn Monroe lunchboxes, Elvis Presley paraphernalia, Route 66 mementos, and many other obscure items.

Another old-fashioned soda fountain is Fosselman's Ice Cream Co., which opened in 1919 and churns its own ice cream onsite. 1824 W Main St., Alhambra.

—1922

OLDEST OUTDOOR ATHLETIC STADIUM
ROSE BOWL STADIUM
1001 Rose Bowl Dr., Pasadena

Each New Year's Day, the Rose Bowl Game follows the Tournament of Roses Parade at the Rose Bowl Stadium. It was built specifically for the Rose Bowl Game (first played in 1902, and America's oldest college football postseason bowl game) and national collegiate football.

A Pasadena landmark and home to UCLA Bruin Football, the stadium also hosts Americafest Fourth of July Celebration, concerts, religious services, filmings, and the world's largest flea market. It was also the site for the 1932 and 1984 Olympic Games, five NFL Super Bowl games, the 1994 Men's World Cup, and the 1999 Women's World Cup.

The original stadium was horseshoe-shaped and required 28 miles of lumber for the 57,000-seat viewing stands. The Rose Bowl Stadium was expanded several times over the years and became a bowl when the southern stands were completed in 1928. In the 1940s and 1950s the stadium was used for auto racing, and more recently it has hosted swap meets.

The Rose Bowl Stadium underwent a decades-long renovation that added many upgrades, such as a new video scoreboard, LED lighting, wider pedestrian tunnels, and improved seating configurations. The Rose Bowl Stadium, the

Home to the historic Rose Bowl Game, the Rose Bowl Stadium hosts various events. Photo courtesy of Los Angeles Tourism & Convention Board

host for the 2022 Super Bowl, currently has a seating capacity of 90,888.

Originally designed by architect Myron Hunt, the Rose Bowl Stadium is recognized as a US National Historic Landmark and a California Historic Civil Engineering Landmark.

The stadium offers several public tours that visit the original 1922 locker room, press box, luxury suites, court of champions, and the iconic field.

Adjacent to the stadium, the government-owned Brookside Golf Course is among the oldest in L.A. County. It opened with nine holes in 1925 and expanded to two 18-hole courses. Brookside also hosts on-site music festivals and various community events. "We're leading the way for golf courses to offer more than golfing," said Brookside Municipal Golf Operations Advisor David Sams.

Oldest Women's Sanitarium

Rockhaven Sanitarium Historic District

2713 Honolulu Ave., Glendale

Tucked away in a residential neighborhood, Rockhaven Sanitarium sits eerily quiet, its cottages vacant among neglected gardens.

Inside, it's a time capsule, with 1930s tiles and built-in furniture. Faded photographs, rosaries, and clothing are reminders of the mentally ill women who once lived here.

Originally made of local rock but later rebuilt after the 1971 earthquake, Rockhaven was founded in 1923 by psychiatric nurse Agnes Richards as an antidote to the prison-like asylums of the time. She created a place where women with mental illness or dementia could be treated with dignity and respect. Women were called residents or ladies, not patients. Richards pioneered a holistic approach to mental illness through art, occupational therapy, social activities, and outings.

"Back then, women with mental illness were held in horrific situations. And not just mentally ill women. If a husband didn't want to be burdened by a divorce, he could ask a pharmacist for a prescription to commit his wife to a mental institution," said Mike Lawler, a local historian and author.

As the number of Rockhaven residents grew, Richards bought surrounding houses to create a compound of 14 buildings on

For many years Rockhaven Sanitarium was home to women with mental illness. Photo courtesy of Glendale Public Library

3.5 acres. The homelike setting had lush gardens, pathways, and courtyards. In front, a fountain nestling a Gladding McBean statue, *Reclining Nude*, is known as Rockhaven's symbol—the Lady of Rockhaven.

Between 80 to 120 women lived in Rockhaven at a time in private bedrooms, shared bedrooms, or dorm-style buildings. A wealthy woman could rent an entire house. The nurse-to-patient ratio was high.

Residents included Marilyn Monroe's mother, Gladys Pearl Baker (who once tied bedsheets together to climb out a closet window), and Billie Burke (Glinda in *The Wizard of Oz*).

In the 1960s and 1970s, when psychotherapeutic drugs became available to treat mental illness, Rockhaven phased in women with dementia and Alzheimer's Disease.

Until 2001 Rockhaven was family operated, with Richards' granddaughter, Patricia Traviss, in charge. Rockhaven changed ownership a few times until the City of Glendale bought the former women's sanitarium in 2008, and accepted an $8 million grant from the State of California in 2021to build a library or museum about mental health.

Rockhaven Sanitarium is listed on the State and National Registries of Historic Resources.

The 501c(3) nonprofit, Friends of Rockhaven supports Rockhaven Park by raising funds to help the City of Glendale with preservation efforts. It also conducts property tours, organizes community events, and creates volunteer opportunities.

Oldest
Nature Center
San Dimas Nature Center
628 N Sycamore Canyon Rd., San Dimas

About 28 miles from downtown L.A., the 128-acre natural space hugs the foothills of the San Gabriel Mountains. When the County of Los Angeles first purchased these parklands in 1909, it was known as the San Dimas Quarry. In 1925, the county converted the lands to form the San Dimas Foothill Park. Subsequent purchases of additional parcels in 1943, 1949, 1957, and 1959 expanded the public park to its current size.

Around 1930, a small white house was built as the residence for the San Dimas water tank operator, Percy Conklin. He became the park's superintendent, while his daughter Evelyn served as a recreation services leader. Avid naturalists, they educated visitors about ecosystems, wildlife, and the canyon's history. In the outdoor areas, they built a small wildlife sanctuary that focused on wildlife and rehabilitation. The animal sanctuary is home to indigenous Southern California animals that can no longer live in their natural habitats, due to injuries and other reasons.

The natural space was renamed the San Dimas Community Regional Park in 1949. The area was home to species including bobcats, coyotes, red foxes, porcupines, deer, raccoons, birds,

The San Dimas Nature Center has hiking trails and is home to wildlife. Photo courtesy of Jason Sandoval

reptiles, and other animals. The current nature center facility broke ground in 1999 and opened in 2000, adjacent to the historic white house. The nature center offers programs, storytelling, and hiking.

Several trails meander through the park. A one-mile, self-guided trail loop begins in an oak woodland, follows a pine grove, and climbs into chaparral-covered foothills.

OLDEST SEARCH AND RESCUE

Montrose

With its numerous hiking trails, picnic areas, and campgrounds, the Los Angeles National Forest is a fun getaway for locals and visitors. But with winding roads, deep ravines, and a maze of hiking trails, it's also where many people get lost, injured, drive off the mountainside, or get stuck in snow.

And when these accidents happen, the Montrose Search and Rescue Team—one of eight nonprofit volunteer rescue teams affiliated with the Los Angeles County Sheriff's Department— jumps into action.

Originally known as the Montrose Mountaineers, the Montrose Search and Rescue Team was started in 1947 by a group of Civilian Air Defense members to help those lost or injured in the local mountains. But it traces its beginnings to World War II. In 1942, just after Pearl Harbor, the Montrose Sheriff Station was designated as the headquarters for the Air Raid Wardens program. As attacks became less likely, the team focused on mountain rescues. These missions were so successful that when the war ended, L.A. County reformed them into auxiliary deputy sheriffs, with an official mission as a "disaster law enforcement organization."

At the same time, construction began on the Los Angeles Crest Highway, which carves deep into the wilderness and

Montrose Search and Rescue volunteers have saved the lives of thousands of people injured in the Angeles National Forest. Photos courtesy of Montrose Search and Rescue

was eventually completed in 1956. In 1947, the Lions Club bought the team a Jeep and a trailer filled with rescue supplies. The volunteers were deputized in 1950 and named the Sheriff Emergency Reserve Team.

A growing number of calls due to more car crashes and lost hikers led to the official formation of the Montrose Search and Rescue Team in 1965. The men and women of the team are trained to respond to virtually any wilderness emergency, 24 hours a day. Averaging between 130-162 calls per year, Montrose Search and Rescue is one of the busiest teams in the county.

To join the team, volunteers—who come from various professions, including teaching, nursing, and engineering—must pass the rigorous mountaineering and rescue training program. In addition, they must obtain an EMT license, and apply to become a reserve deputy sheriff.

The Altadena Mountain Rescue Group is another volunteer-based organization that responds to emergencies in the Angeles National Forest. Established in 1951, the Altadena Mountain Rescue Team has been a member unit of the Sheriff's Department Reserve Forces Bureau since 1956.

Oldest Children's Bookstore
Once Upon a Time Bookstore
2207 Honolulu Ave., Montrose

The Palacios family, owners of the Once Upon a Time Bookstore, has a happily-ever-after tale to tell. After all, if not for them the store might not be here today. The children's bookstore was the family's neighborhood bookstore, founded in 1966 by local mom and artist Jane Humphrey. It's where Maureen Palacios's daughters Jessica and Amelia bought their favorite books.

So, when Jane Humphrey decided to retire and sell the store in April 2003, they were devastated. Especially when no one offered to buy it. Worried about the store's fate, Jessica—nine years old at the time—wrote a letter to the *Los Angeles Times*, asking, "Where will I find my fifth Harry Potter book if there is no 'Once Upon A Time'?"

Maureen, who had worked in human resources for 20 years, and  her husband decided to buy the store. Friends and family expressed concern about buying a bookstore at a time when online

The family-owned Once Upon a Time Bookstore has a happy story to share.

book sales were crushing independent bookstores. But the Palacioses did their homework, learning retail and pursuing their dream.

Maureen Palacios and her daughter Jessica, who plays a big role in the family business.

Following Jane Humphrey's advice, they chatted with customers, kept notes about their literary interests, and got to know their customers. Each year, sales increased.

And over the years, despite challenges that included a rent increase facilitating a move across the street, Maureen's medical issues, and the COVID-19 pandemic, Once Upon a Time survived.

In the meantime, Jessica, now grown, became the buyer and store manager. The staff is composed of local youth who grew up visiting the store. Maureen Palacios credits the success to the store's window displays, promotions of local authors, author signings, in-store events, a steady fan base, and the store's high-profile location on a walkable street. The store is organized by age and themes, with books facing out to get noticed. "We want to please and excite the eye," said Maureen Palacios. "We tend to have a story. We sell dreams. You have to get people to see the story and want that book."

The bookstore, which has won many awards and accolades, is known for curating a good selection of diverse books for children and adults.

At the front of the store is a child-sized red barn, inherited from Jane Humphrey, that holds stacks of books and doubles as a play area. And on hand to greet customers is Pippi, the family's cat.

SAN FERNANDO VALLEY

OLDEST SHEET MUSIC STORE
BAXTER NORTHUP MUSIC CO.
14534 Ventura Blvd., Sherman Oaks

Many local music students who have taken lessons privately or in school, or played in a garage band, have probably shopped at Baxter Northup Music Co., the oldest continuously operating music store in California. The music shop specializes in sheet music, brass and woodwind instrument sales, and rentals and repairs, in addition to offering lessons.

The shop was founded in 1906 in downtown L.A. by flutist Harry Baxter. Not much is known about Ray Northup, a silent partner. The store moved to Ventura Boulevard in the San Fernando Valley in the 1950s and has been at its present address since 1993. The current owners bought the shop 40 years ago.

From local garage bands to professional musicians, and students and teachers, the shop has something for everyone. The store is filled with an assortment of instruments and accessories, but it's the rows and rows of sheet music that are most impressive. And it's what distinguishes the music store from others. That, and the quality of the instruments.

Owner Ed Walker prides himself on selling top-quality, new and used instruments for beginning, intermediate, and professional players. The shop has a large inventory of flutes, clarinets, trumpets, trombones, saxophones, violins, cellos, and more it rents to students. The instruments are provided by the Music & Arts Company. Baxter Northup has a full, in-house repair shop. A variety of music lessons are offered on-site.

A few miles away, the Valley Relics Museum (located at the Van Nuys Airport) is a unique pop culture facility that collects vintage neon signs, classic cars, yearbooks, restaurant menus, art, BMX bikes, and many other memorabilia from the San Fernando Valley. 7900 Balboa Blvd., Van Nuys.

Baxter Northup rents, sells, and repairs instruments but is best known for its extensive selection of sheet music.

─────────────────────────────────────1912

OLDEST COSTUME COMPANY

WESTERN COSTUME COMPANY

11041 Vanowen St., North Hollywood

With eight miles of costumes in a 120,000-squre-foot building, Western Costume Company is a one-stop shop for costume designers, costumers and stylists—who make up about 85 percent of the business. The rest are schools, theaters, and the general public.

Founded as a production studio by L.L. Burns (a former Benham Indian Trading Company worker with a large collection of Native American costumes), the costume company has been providing period costumes, shoes, and accessories for movies, shows and photo shoots since 1912. And what it doesn't have in stock, it will make. For Dorothy's ruby slippers in *The Wizard of Oz*, the cobbler covered a pair of slippers with sequins and beads.

As the motion picture industry grew, so did the business, which changed ownership several times until it was purchased by Bill Haber in 1989.

Western Costume Company's costumes, which date from the 1820s, have come a long way since the early days, when costume designers could get away with putting zippers in 1800s

The Western Costume Company has been dressing Hollywood since 1912. Photo courtesy of Maria Wessenauer

dresses. Since cameras couldn't see it, it didn't matter. But today, authenticity is everything, and a costume designer wouldn't dream of putting in a zipper where it didn't belong.

To create authentic costumes, the company has several designated departments, including a dedicated research library, milliner, tailor shop, shoe shop, armor room, jewelry shop, and more.

In 2012, the Costume Designers Guild presented Western Costume with a special Service Award honoring the company's 100 years of professional contributions, from the silent era to the present. Appointments are necessary to visit the store.

Nearby, tours to see a collection of vintage clothing, artifacts, and historic buildings are available at the San Fernando Valley Historical Society, housed in the historic Andres Pico Adobe. 10940 Sepulveda Blvd., Mission Hills.

The Western Costume Company has costumes from the 1820s.
Photo courtesy of the Western Costume Company

OLDEST THEME PARK
UNIVERSAL STUDIOS HOLLYWOOD
100 Universal City Plaza, Universal City

U niversal Studios Hollywood, a working studio and movie-
based theme park, opened its doors to the public in 1964.
But its history dates to March 15,1915 when film producer
and Universal Studios founder Carl Laemmle held a grand
opening for Universal City, a self-contained movie-making
community built on a 230-acre chicken farm.

He began offering tours of his film studio called Universal City
to the general public for 25 cents (plus an extra five cents for a
boxed chicken lunch). People could watch live performances
and tapings, and visit an onsite zoo. The original tour was
discontinued in 1930 with the introduction of sound films, which
required a quiet set. Soundstages weren't yet soundproofed.

Universal Studios Hollywood is both a working studio and theme park with a fun behind-the-scenes tour.

It wasn't until July 1964 that Universal Studios reopened as a theme park with rides and a behind-the-scenes studio tour. Tickets, then $2.50, were sold from a temporary trailer on Lankershim Boulevard. The 90-minute tours featured pink-and-white-striped Glamor Trams that brought guests around the studio's backlot to see costumes designed by Edith Head, a makeup demonstration, a star's dressing room, and a western stunt show.

As more entertainment was added to the tour, and to keep labor costs down, Universal began using audience volunteers to interact in scenes. Around the same time, fixed attractions with special effects joined the tour. The first was the Flash Flood set (still there today), where 20,000 gallons of water rushes 200 feet through a Mexican village street toward the tram—which makes a quick getaway.

Universal Studios Hollywood evolved into two split levels—upper and lower, which are connected by a series of escalators called the Starway. As of 2021, Universal Studios Hollywood contains 10 themed, immersive rides, seven live shows, and two play areas. Each lot features rides, shows, and attractions in addition to food, beverage, and merchandise shops. The signature 45- to 60-minute Studio Tour, which visits various backlot sets and sound stages, is still the main attraction.

Thousands of people attended Universal City's grand opening on March 15, 1915. Two days of festivities included a parade, western stunt show, and a simulated flash flood attraction. Tragically, a stunt pilot was killed in a weather-related crash on the second day.

1945

Oldest Rectangular, Thin Crust Pizza
Barone's
Several locations

Many pizzerias claim to be the first, but what sets Barone's apart is the rectangular, thin crust, Neapolitan pizza the family says it introduced and served to L.A. in the old Casa de Cadillac building from 1945 to 1949 before moving to another location.

"There were two reasons for the rectangular shape. One, it was a more efficient way to put more pizza in the oven. And two, back in the 1940s, these pans were cheaper, and that's all they could afford," said Michael Monteleone, owner of the Barone's in Thousand Oaks, one of several Barone's locations that include Woodland Hills and Van Nuys.

To this day, the pizza recipe and rectangular shape have stayed the same in all the Barone's restaurants. For over half a century the restaurant has been a family affair, starting with several Monteleone siblings, most notably Frank Monteleone, who made Barone's what it is today.

"Through the years, family members pitched in with cooking the secret family recipes, which were derived from their grandparents from Sicily and Naples," said Monteleone, who never worked in the restaurant but invested in it to keep it going.

Sine 1945 Barone's Pizza continues the family tradition of baking rectangular, thin crust pizza. Photo courtesy of Barone's Pizza

Although Barone's pizza and Italian dressing are the restaurant's top sellers, the menu includes many Italian dishes.

Barone's pizza is made with a blend of recipes from six related Italian families who created the original Barone's Italian restaurant.

OLDEST CHILI HOUSE
CHILI JOHN'S
2018 W Burbank Blvd., Burbank

S teve Hager didn't grow up in the food business, but good fortune handed him and his wife, Claudine, the oldest operating restaurant in Burbank (1946) that also happens to serve the oldest chili recipe on record, dating to 1902.

Not only that, "this is the official chili of the Green Bay Packers," said Hager. The connection to Green Bay, Wisconsin began with Lithuanian immigrant John Isaac, who was first serving his Southwestern chili from a chuckwagon in 1900 before opening a bar in Green Bay. He borrowed $40 to have the name Chili John's trademarked in 1902, making it one of the oldest trademarks in the registry.

Meanwhile, the chili became so popular that he opened a Chili John's restaurant 13 years later. Made with rendered fat that congeals at room temperature, giving it a unique oily texture, the chili isn't meant to be eaten straight. Similar to a spaghetti sauce but with its own special spice, it's poured over spaghetti or burgers and hot dogs, said Hager. Isaac is also credited with inventing oyster crackers. "He wanted them small to soak up the oil from the chili."

In 1946, Isaac's son, Ernie, moved to Los Angeles and opened

Chili John's makes the oldest chili recipe on record.

Chili John's chili is derived from a recipe in Green Bay, Wisconsin. Photo courtesy of Steve Hager

Chili John's restaurant in Burbank near the studios and Lockheed Aircraft Company (which later moved from Burbank). He installed the U-shaped counter and painted a mountain lake mural along one wall—both of which remain in place today.

Hager's wife's family bought the retro-style diner in 1989, and four years ago sold the business to their daughter and son-in-law. The couple sticks to the original chili recipe, which is quite the process.

Hager, who chops the meat, said they use beef suet, a fat deposit near the cow's kidneys. They render that and clarify it before adding it to the in-house-ground shoulder meat. Then spices are added. It takes about 20-24 hours to cook. It is oil-based and has no water left by the end of the process, and almost no sugar content, making it safe to store at room temperature.

In addition to the original chili recipe, they added chicken and turkey chili to the menu. They also make turducken chili served with stuffing made with fresh cranberries. Chili John's also offers a vegetarian option, so there's something for every palate.

Of historical significance is the nearby Warner Bros. Studios, established nearly 100 years ago. The studio offers customized, behind-the-scenes tours that begin with a short video about Warner Bros. before guests board small, open-air trams to view locations for numerous old and new productions, including the mock French street where Humphrey Bogart courted Ingrid Bergman in Casablanca.

SANTA CLARITA VALLEY

OLDEST GOLD DISCOVERY SITE
PLACERITA CANYON STATE PARK
19152 Placerita Canyon Rd., Newhall

Placerita Canyon is known for wildlife and hiking trails, but it's also the site of the first gold discovery in California. The discovery of gold in Sutter's Mill in Northern California, which often gets credit for the discovery of gold, actually happened six years after gold was found in Santa Clarita Valley.

In 1842, rancher Francisco Lopez was herding cattle and hunting for game with two men on his niece's ranch in what is now called Placerita Canyon in the Santa Clarita Valley, 35 miles north of today's downtown L.A. They stopped for lunch, where Lopez fell asleep under the shade of an oak tree and dreamed he was floating in a pool of liquid gold.

After waking up, Lopez used his sheath knife to dig up some wild onions and saw little nuggets of gold clinging to the roots. Lopez's discovery sparked California's first gold rush.

Hundreds of prospectors flocked to Santa Clarita to try their luck. An average of about 260 pounds of the metal annually was mined from the valley during the boom years, between 1842 and 1847.

The tree where Lopez reportedly had his golden nap is still there and is called "The Oak of The Golden Dream." The old, gnarled, coast live oak is near the Placerita Canyon Nature Center.

The Oak of the Golden Dream at Placerita Canyon State Park is the site of the first gold discovery in California.

The short, paved Heritage Trail leads to the tree. Along the way, there's a tunnel featuring murals that depict the history of the canyon, from natural habitat to California Indian homestead to ranch. The last panel reads, "A Dream Come True: Gold!"

Placerita Canyon Natural Area is a 350-acre wildlife sanctuary with a nature center, hiking trails, and a seasonal stream and waterfall. Another on-site landmark is the Walker Cabin, built by the area's first homesteader, Frank Walker, around 1920 for his family. 19152 Placerita Canyon Rd., Newhall

Oldest Oil Boomtown
Mentryville
27201 Pico Canyon Rd., Newhall

Tucked away in Newhall's chaparral slopes in the Santa Susana Mountains, Mentryville was an oil-drilling boomtown from 1876 to 1900. The town was built around oil well Pico No. 4, the first commercially successful oil well in the western United States. Today, Mentryville is a ghost town, home to historic buildings that include a 13-room mansion called Pico Cottage, a one-room red schoolhouse, and a period barn. Mentryville and Pico No. 4 are registered as California State Historical Landmarks.

The town is named after French immigrant Charles Alexander Mentry, the oil well's driller, and later, superintendent of the company that would become Chevron. Around July 1876, Mentry set up Pico No. 4 for drilling. Later, on September 26, he expanded the well by digging an extra 300 feet. While digging, Mentry discovered a massive deposit of oil which shot out of the derrick 60 feet into the air. Pico No. 4 was the longest continually operating oil well in the world, closing in 1990.

The town, then called Pico Springs, had bunkhouses, cabins, a schoolhouse, bakery, and dance hall. Mentry's mansion had four fireplaces and three bathrooms. The town was the first in Santa Clarita to have natural gas lighting. About 200 families lived there at one point.

After Mentry's death on October 4, 1900, the town slowly went into decline. Much of the oil had been depleted and field workers left. By 1932, there were about six families living in Mentryville.

Although secluded, Mentryville is easily accessible by vehicle. It's a great location for filmmakers, history buffs, and hikers.

Among Newhall's many historic sites is the hilltop William S. Hart Museum, showcasing the 166-acre ranch of the 1920s original silent film cowboy. The 22-room mansion contains Hart's personal belongings and art collection. The ranch is located in Hart Park, home to a herd of American bison, hiking trails, and a picnic area. 24151 Newhall Ave., Newhall.

Mentryville, the site of a booming oil town in 1876, is now a ghost town.

OLDEST RESTAURANT
THE ORIGINAL SAUGUS CAFE
25861 Railroad Ave., Santa Clarita

O ften during a meal at The Original Saugus Cafe (simply called Saugus Cafe), a train goes rumbling by, but no one seems to mind. It's a reminder that the restaurant got its start as a railroad rest stop in 1886. And it helps that the diner's classic American comfort food and service are good. Plus, it's always been a gathering place for locals discussing the news of the day.

When James Herbert Tolfree opened the "Saugus Eating House," its location at the north end of the Saugus Rail Depot made it a handy stop for a bite to eat. The train station, named after Saugus, Massachusetts (the birthplace of local developer Henry Newhall), was a stop on the Southern Pacific Railroad connecting Los Angeles with San Francisco. The cafe adopted the station's name.

Throughout its history, the cafe has fed many dignitaries and celebrities, including two US presidents. On April 25, 1891, President Benjamin Harrison stopped by for a meal; and in May 1903, President Theodore Roosevelt was served a New York steak. About a year later, Los Angeles Aqueduct builder William Mulholland and Los Angeles Mayor Fred Eaton met for a breakfast meeting at the cafe.

In 1905, the cafe moved across the street from the rail station to its current location. In the meantime, the area was becoming a popular location for Hollywood films (especially westerns),

The Original Saugus Cafe has been feeding people since 1886.

prompting the cafe's remodel in 1916. Directors John Ford and D. W. Griffith, and actors Douglas Fairbanks, Mary Pickford, John Wayne, and Clark Gable, were among the celebrities who dined at the cafe.

While the old-school diner has been renovated over the years, it retains a homey ambiance. The eatery has wood floors, newspaper clippings on the wall, and daily specials handwritten on a board. The names of longtime employees and close friends are stitched onto counter seats. There's an attached bar at the far end of the diner with more seating.

Saugus Cafe offers an extensive breakfast, lunch, and dinner menu. Traditional breakfast items include omelettes, pancakes, crepes, and the house specialty: chicken fried steak and eggs. Burgers, sandwiches, and salads are available on the lunch menu; and dinner options include steaks, meatloaf, and spaghetti and meatballs. Diners can count on generous portions, sensible prices, and down-home hospitality.

In the cafe's early days, the only building in Saugus was the train depot, with the possible exception of a blacksmith shop at the present corner of Magic Mountain Pkwy and San Fernando Rd. Local cowboys would allegedly take "pot shots" at the station and passing northbound trains.

OLDEST STILL-STANDING JAILHOUSE

OLD NEWHALL JAIL

24522 Spruce St. Newhall

I t's hard to imagine that the small, forlorn building adjacent to the modern Old Town Newhall Library was once a jailhouse. But that it was. And the barred windows do kind of give it away.

Plans for the jailhouse began in 1888, when the County of Los Angeles gave constable John Howe (a lawman since 1878) a place to lock up prisoners. The proposed location for the new jail was on county-owned property at the end of Arch Street in Newhall.

Now a vacant building, the Old Newhall Jail is located adjacent to the Old Town Newhall Library.

However, that didn't sit well with Newhall train stationmaster John T. Gifford, who didn't want criminals next door to his family home. So, he bought a parcel at 1026 Spruce Street for $68 and negotiated with the county to swap the land. While that business arrangement may have taken place earlier, county records show Gifford signed the property over to the county in 1905.

Architectural plans called for the construction of a concrete building with a 1/4-inch-thick steel door covering. Construction was completed by May 1906, when the windows were covered with heavy screens and the interior walls were whitewashed. In 1929, the building was appraised for the first time at a sum of $2,000.

Until 1926, it was used as the jail and constable's office. The jail housed approximately 250 prisoners from January through October of 1939. After that time, it was no longer used. Since then, it has housed various commercial businesses, including a florist. The structure retains the original barred windows. For now, the jailhouse remains locked up.

The western-themed Old Town Newhall is home to historic sites and attractions. The Walk of Western Stars features bronze- and terrazzo-stamped tiles honoring Roy Rogers, John Wayne, Gene Autry, Steve McQueen, Robert Conrad, Jimmy Stewart, and many others.

OLDEST DAM DISASTER
ST. FRANCIS DAM
San Francisquito Canyon

The collapse of the St. Francis Dam, considered to be one of the worst American civil engineering disasters of the 20th century, claimed the lives of at least 431 people and destroyed the career of William Mulholland, the dam's designer.

The 180-foot-high, 600-foot-long concrete structure was designed and built between 1924 and 1926 in San Francisquito Canyon (about 40 miles northwest of downtown L.A.), by the Los Angeles Department of Water and Power, then named the Bureau

of Water Works and Supply. Mulholland, also credited with building the Los Angeles Aqueduct, was the department's general manager and chief engineer.

Cracks and minor leaks were expected in a dam as large as the St. Francis.

Chunks of the collapsed St. Francis Dam can be seen on a trail in San Francisquito Canyon.

But dam keeper Tony Harnischfeger was concerned about the brownish runoff he saw, and reported it to Mulholland on the morning of March 12, 1928. Mulholland and his chief engineer, Harvey Van Norman, inspected the dam, and concluding it was safe, returned to Los Angeles.

At 11:57 p.m. on March 12, 1928, the dam collapsed and unleashed a 250-foot wall of water (about 12.4 billion gallons) and mudflow that rushed down the canyon and into the Santa Clara River, wiping out about 1,200 homes and hundreds of people, many swept into the Pacific Ocean.

Investigations later revealed the dam had been built on unstable soil. Chunks of the dam can still be seen along the closed portion of San Francisquito Canyon Road. In May 2019, the area was officially designated a national monument to protect what's left of the ruins.

The Iron Horse Bridge, a railroad trestle bridge built in 1898, was moved to its current location over the Santa Clara River after the St. Francis Dam broke in 1928. In 2012, the City of Santa Clarita dedicated a four-mile Iron Horse trail that connects to the South Fork Trail. 25311 Magic Mountain Pkwy.

SANTA CATALINA ISLAND

OLDEST HOTEL
GLENMORE PLAZA HOTEL
118 Summer Ave., Avalon

Built on the heels of the landmark Hotel del Coronado in San Diego in 1891, the Victorian-style Glenmore Plaza Hotel was among the few buildings to survive the 1915 fire that destroyed much of Avalon, the one-square-mile town (and the island's only town).

Located on a side street near the beach, the comfortable, unassuming hotel has been renovated with modern features, including pillowtop beds and marble bathrooms (originally, the hotel had shared bathrooms), yet retains old-school features, such as actual room keys embossed with the hotel's name and image.

There are no elevators, and stairs lead to hallways that zigzag through the hotel to guestrooms. Some have balconies with peekaboo ocean views; others face a courtyard. The hotel has hosted many celebrities, such as Clark Gable, Marilyn Monroe, Charlie Chaplin, Theodore Roosevelt and Amelia Earhart. Some have suites named after them. The largest suite is named after Clark Gable, who stayed at the hotel in the 1920s and '30s.

But things soon took a dramatic turn. During WWII, Catalina was

The Glenmore Plaza Hotel uses sturdy room keys.

The quaint Glenmore Plaza Hotel is the sister hotel of the famous Hotel del Coronado in San Diego.

occupied by the US military, and the hotel, along with others, was used by the US Maritime Service to house trainees. Then, during the 1960s and 1970s, the hotel fell into disrepair. Nevertheless, Jack Amoroso and his sons, James and Jack Jr., saw the property's potential and purchased it in 1981. The hotel was extensively renovated in the 1980s, and again a few years ago.

The Glenmore offers a free shuttle to and from the boat terminal (although the short, scenic walk along the waterfront is quite nice).

Built in 1925, the Catalina Chimes Tower was presented as a gift to the town of Avalon by Mrs. Ada Wrigley. The chimes, which have been tolling on the quarter of the hour between 8 a.m. and 8 p.m. since 1925, can be heard throughout town.

Oldest Fishing Club
Tuna Club
100 St. Catherine Way, Avalon

Charles Frederick Holder, a biologist, author, and sportsman, introduced rod and reel fishing with linen line as a more humane way than nets to catch big game fish. After his historic catch of a 183-pound bluefin tuna using a rod and reel with a linen line, he formed the private membership Tuna Club with an emphasis on conservation on June 15, 1898.

The club was open to men who agreed to follow the strict rules of fish engagement and who promoted fish conservation. The club's articles of incorporation were finalized on July 20, 1898, and three membership classifications were outlined: Honorary, Associate, and Active. For a time, the front door had a sign that read, "no women," but that was axed by the island's first female mayor, Irene Strobel, in 1982.

Some of the earlier honorary members included C. B. DeMille, President Herbert Hoover, Charlie Chaplin, and Winston Churchill, who apparently was a lucky angler. Shortly after his arrival, he caught a 188-pound marlin, and reeled it in in 20 minutes. After Churchill returned to England, he had a fishing gaffe engraved and sent to the Tuna Club as a thank-you gift. It remains on display in the clubhouse.

Currently, the club has 183 members. The rules to join remain the same. A person needs to be sponsored by an existing member, catch a qualifying fish, be approved by the board, and pay the fee.

The Tuna Club, a private members club that practices conservation, is the oldest fishing club in the world.

"There's very little change; we stick to tradition," said manager John Talsky, a boat captain for 20 years.

The club holds six tournaments a year and about one monthly event from June to September. Local fish include tuna, marlin, and broadbill swordfish. Members are allowed to keep some fish, but mostly they practice catch and release. "It's more of a sporting thing, not taking volumes of fish," said Talsky.

Members have 24/7 access to the two-story clubhouse—the second in its history. A desk in the Hotel Metropole served as club headquarters from 1898 to 1908. The first clubhouse was a gift from the Banning brothers, owners and founders of the Santa Catalina Island Company, in 1908. It burned down in 1915. To save as many trophies and memorabilia as possible, members threw them in the water (and later retrieved them).

The new clubhouse, completed in 1916, contains a women's lounge (added after 1946), a library with trophies, vintage rods and reels, and a card room with historical photos and documents. The second floor contains bedrooms and showers.

The Tuna Club is a California Historical Landmark and is on the National Register of Historic Places.

Another Catalina landmark, the Queen Ann architectural-style Holly Hill House was completed in 1890 on the hill overlooking Avalon Bay. Peter Gano, a retired civil engineer from Pasadena, purchased the prime section of land in the new City of Avalon in 1888 to build his home.

OLDEST FAMILY-OWNED BOAT COMPANY
MISS CATALINA SPEEDBOAT/CATALINA EXPRESS
Long Beach, San Pedro, and Dana Point ports

It took Al Bombard about four hours to sail the 22 miles from the mainland in Los Angeles to Catalina Island in 1919. He fell in love with Catalina, moved his family there, and established a boating business.

Utilizing his skills as a mechanic in the auto racing industry, Bombard designed and built six Miss Catalina speedboats, customizing the engines from World War I Liberty airplane engines. The speedboats, which traveled at speeds up to 55 miles per hour, operated from 1921 to around 1958.

During that time, they were used to transport film from movies made on the island back to the mainland. But they were mostly known for providing joyrides for island visitors. The most exciting ride, called "Meet the Steamer," greeted the SS *Catalina*, a 301-foot steamship that was the main form of transportation between Los Angeles and Catalina from 1924 to 1975.

For a few years, the only way to reach the island was via a two-hour boat ride with Catalina Cruises or by plane. The Bombard family started Catalina Express in 1981 to transport passengers more quickly. Doug Bombard (who grew up working on the speedboats), his son Greg, and longtime colleague Tom Rutter retrofitted a 56-foot charter fishing boat, and customized the

Al Bombard designed and built six Miss Catalina Speedboats. Photo courtesy of Catalina Express

interior with airline-style cabin seating. The modified vessel with turbocharged diesel engines made the trip in 90 minutes.

Throughout the 1980s Catalina Express worked with boat builders to design monohull vessels that carried more passengers.

In the 1990s, Catalina Express launched additional customized monohulls, including the Avalon Express, Catalina Express, and Islander Express, and acquired its first two catamarans.

By the early 2000s, the ferry company had two more catamarans—Catalina Jet and Jet Cat Express. In addition, the company started to re-engineer the fleet to reduce greenhouse emissions to the Environmental Protection Agency's Tier II and Tier III marine regulations.

Catalina Express currently has a fleet of eight vessels that transport passengers in about 60 minutes from Long Beach, San Pedro, and Dana Point to Avalon and Two Harbors on Catalina Island.

Boats sail to Two Harbors, where Civil War Barracks were built in 1864 to house "militant" Native Americans. Native Americans were never interned on Catalina, but the barracks remain as a monument to the Civil War and WWII. Movies such as Mutiny on the Bounty were produced on Catalina in the 1920s and 1930s, and the barracks provided lodging to moviemakers as they filmed on sets imitating a South Pacific island. The barracks are managed by the Isthmus Yacht Club.

Oldest Circular Ballroom
Catalina Casino
1 Casino Way, Avalon

Catalina Casino is Catalina Island's most recognized structure, easily visible from a distance while approaching via boat. It's easy to imagine the excitement the early visitors felt as they sailed the 22 miles from the mainland to the island, dressed in their best for lavish shows and parties in the new casino building, completed on May 29, 1929.

Built in just 14 months under the direction of chewing gum magnate William Wrigley Jr. and David M. Renton as an entertainment facility, it was named casino, which means gathering place in Italian. (It was never a gambling casino.) The 10-story casino (the height of the building is equal to a 12-story building) cost $2 million to build.

The ground level, 1,200-seat, Avalon movie theater was the first to be designed specifically for "talkies" (films with sound). Although designed for movies, it also has a full stage, orchestra pit, and dressing rooms for stage productions. The foyer is paneled in black walnut under a beamed, barrel ceiling with 88 gold stars and 22-karat gold leaf trim. The theater's dome ceiling with twinkling stars, and materials between the ceiling and walls, provide excellent acoustics.

Catalina Casino is the island's largest and most recognizable building.

Ramps, instead of stairs, were installed to move large groups of people faster to the 20,000-foot-ballroom and promenade on the top level. It's the world's largest circular ballroom, accommodating 3,000 dancers. The 180-foot-diameter dance floor is made with maple, white oak, and rosewood in a16-sided pattern converging toward a central circle. A balcony encircling the building offers expansive island and ocean views.

The casino is also remarkable for its artwork, overseen by Los Angeles artist John Gabriel Beckman. The exterior features a large mural with nine underwater scenes painted by five artists, who painted themselves in Art Deco murals inside the theater.In its heyday, the casino attracted Big Band-era names and performers, such as Danny Kaye, Kate Smith, and Ronald Reagan. Wrigley had a private viewing room above the theater. Today, it's still used for special events and celebrations.

The towering 80-foot Wrigley Memorial, in the Catalina Island Conservancy Botanic Garden, honors the memory of chewing gum entrepreneur William Wrigley Jr., who bought most of Catalina in 1919 and invested millions in developing the island. The garden showcases the island's endemic plants.

SOURCES

Oldest Los Angeles District: elpueblo.lacity.org

Oldest Standing House: elpueblo.lacity.org

Oldest Plaza: nps.gov/nr/travel/ca/ca12.htm

Oldest Church in the City of Los Angeles: laplacita.org; elpueblo.lacity.org

Oldest Surviving Brick House: elpueblo. lacity.org

Oldest Surviving Theater Building: laconservancy.org/locations/merced-theatre; Pitt, Leonard; Pitt, Dale, *Los Angeles A-Z, An Encyclopedia of the City and County,* University of California Press, Berkeley and Los Angeles, California, 2000, pg. 321

Oldest Firehouse: elpueblo.lacity.org/ history-el-pueblo

Oldest Surviving Chinese Structure: camla. org/the-building

Oldest Historic Landmark: laconservancy. org/locations/bradbury-building; discoverlosangeles.com/things-to-do/ bradbury-building

Oldest Public Art Sculpture: publicartinla. com/Downtown/figueroa/Pershing_Square/ spanish_american_war_survey.html; onbunkerhill.org/spanish-american-war-memorial-1

Oldest Funicular Railway: angelsflight.org; discoverlosangeles.com/visit/angels-flight-the-story-of-an-la-icon

Oldest Confectionery: fugetsu-do.com

Oldest Operating Bar: goldengopherla.com; Moses, Cedd, *The Essential Magic Behind the Bartenders We Love*, Lioncrest Publishing, 2021

Oldest Italian Hall: iamla.org; elpueblo. lacity.org

Oldest French Dip Sandwich Shop: philippes.com

Oldest Operating Pub: colesfrenchdip.com; pouringwithheart.com

Oldest Remaining Orpheum Theatre: palacedowntown.com/history-of-broadway; laconservancy.org/locations/palace-theatre

Oldest Winery: sanantoniowinery.com

Oldest Public Market: grandcentralmarket. com/history; discoverlosangeles.com/eat-drink/the-best-of-grand-central-market

Oldest Flower Market: originallaflowermarket.com; fashiondistrict. org/shop/la-flower-district

Oldest Mexican Marketplace: olvera-street. com/history; elpueblo.lacity.org

Oldest Outdoor Mural: theamericatropical. org; getty.edu/conservation/our_projects/field_ projects/siqueiros/siqueiros_interpret.html

Oldest Bakery: phoenixbakeryinc.com; latimes.com/local/lanow/la-me-phoenix-bakery-turns-20180614-htmlstory.html; Shyong, Frank, July 14, 2018, *As a Storied Chinatown Bakery Four Generations Labor to Learn Lessons of Family*

Oldest Cemetery: evergreencemeteryla. com/about-us; laconservancy.org/locations/ evergreen-cemetery

Oldest Park: historicechopark.org/history-landmarks/places-landmarks/elysian-park; kcet.org/shows/socal-wanderer/how-to-discover-the-wonders-of-elysian-park-by-car

Oldest Bottled Soda Shop: sodapopstop.com

Oldest Museum: theautry.org/visit/mt-washington-campus; laconservancy.org/ locations/southwest-museum

Oldest Library: en.wikipedia.org/wiki/ Vermont_Square_Branch_Library; lapl.org/ branches/vermont-square/history

Oldest Natural History Museum: nhm.org/ experience-nhm; Pitt, Leonard; Pitt, Dale, *Los Angeles A-Z, An Encyclopedia of the City and County*, University of California Press, Berkeley and Los Angeles, California, 2000

Oldest Automobile Dealership: felixchevrolet.
com/felix-chevrolet-the-story-behind-the-
iconic-dealership; dtlaweekly.com/landmark-
car-dealership-felix-chevrolet-celebrates-100-
years, Landmark Car Dealership Felix Chevrolet
Celebrates 100 Years, *Downtown Los Angeles
Weekly*, April 4, 2021

Oldest Themed Restaurant: laconservancy.
org/locations/tam-oshanter; lawrysonline.
com/our-story; lawrysalacart.com/2012/04/01/
tam-oshanter-90-years-counting

Oldest Mexican Restaurant: elcholo.com/
our-history

Oldest Stadium: lacoliseum.com/coliseum-
history; lamcc.lacounty.gov/History Pitt,
Leonard; Pitt, Dale, Los Angeles *A-Z,
An Encyclopedia of the City and County*,
University of California Press, Berkeley and
Los Angeles, California, 2000, pg. 296

Oldest Fossil Dig Site: tarpits.org;
discoverlosangeles.com/things-to-do/la-brea-
tar-pits-museum; britannica.com/place/La-
Brea-Tar-Pits

Oldest Bowling Alley: highlandparkbowl.
com; secretlosangeles.com/highland-park-
bowl/, L.A.'s Oldest Bowling Alley is in
Highland Park and It's a Prohibition-Era
Palace, June 27, 2021

Oldest Farmers Market: farmersmarketla.com/
history; visitcalifornia.com/experience/original-
los-angeles-farmers-market; discoverlosangeles.
com/things-to-do/the-original-farmers-market-
the-story-of-an-la-icon

Oldest Neighborhood Bookstore:
chevaliersbooks.com/copy-of-about;
bookweb.org/news/chevalier's-serves-la-
neighborhood-76-years-34989, Chevalier's
Serves Neighborhood for 76 Years, American
Booksellers Association, Nov. 21, 2016

Oldest Drive-Through Hamburger Stand:
in-n-out.com/history

Oldest Trains: traveltown.org/our-story/
history

**Oldest Continuously Operating Hollywood
Studio:** paramountstudios.com/paramount-
history.html; Pitt, Leonard; Pitt, Dale, Los
Angeles *A-Z, An Encyclopedia of the City
and County*, University of California Press,
Berkeley and Los Angeles, California, 2000,
pgs.381-382

Oldest Frank Lloyd Wright House:
barnsdall.org/hollyhock-house;
franklloydwright.org/site/hollyhock-house;
laconservancy.org/locations/hollyhock-
house; discoverlosangeles.com/things-to-do/
hollyhock-house-the-story-of-an-la-icon,
Frank Lloyd Wright's Hollyhock House: The
Story of an L.A. Icon, July 10, 2019

Oldest Amphitheater: theford.com/about/
the-ford/history; discoverlosangeles.com/
things-to-do/ford-theatres-the-story-of-an-la-
icon, Ford Theatres, the Story of an L.A. Icon,
Discover Los Angeles.com, April 25, 2019

Oldest Outdoor Concert Venue:
hollywoodbowl.com/about/the-bowl/
hollywood-bowl-history; discoverlosangeles.
com/things-to-do/the-hollywood-bowl-the-
story-of-an-la-icon, The Hollywood Bowl,
The Story of an L.A. Icon, Discover Los
Angeles.com, Feb. 26, 2020

Oldest Famous Sign: The Rise, Ruin and
Restoration of Hollywood's Biggest Name,
Hollywood Sign Trust; hollywoodsign.org/
seeing-the-sign

Oldest Hollywood Hotel:
thehollywoodroosevelt.com;
discoverlosangeles.com/hotels/the-
hollywood-roosevelt-hotel-the-story-of-an-
la-icon, The Hollywood Roosevelt Hotel:
The Story of an L.A. Icon, Discover Los
Angeles, com, March 5, 2020; Roman, James,
*Chronicles of Old Los Angeles, Exploring the
Devilish History of the City of Los Angeles*,
Museyon Inc., 2018, pg. 262

Oldest Cosmetic Building:
thehollywoodmuseum.com/about/our-
history-vision

Oldest Hot Dog Stand: pinkshollywood.com/
about-pinks

Oldest Jewish Congregation: wbtla.org/
about/history

Oldest Canals: kcet.org/shows/lost-la/the-
lost-canals-of-venice-of-america, The Los
Canals of Venice of America, KCET, April
15, 2013; visitveniceca.com/2015/07/23/
venice-canals

Oldest Seaside Attractions: pacpark.com/
history-of-the-santa-monica-pier

Oldest Private Art College: otis.edu/history-
timeline

Oldest Airport: Pitt, Leonard; Pitt, Dale, Los Angeles *A-Z, An Encyclopedia of the City and County*, University of California Press, Berkeley and Los Angeles, California, 2000, pg.294; lawa.org/?snav=4234e38e-b21c-4a7c-b066-9c6fe9855cb4

Oldest Public Water Fountain: lovebeverlyhills.com/things-to-do/view/beverly-gardens-park; californiawaters.com/portfolio/featured-case-studies/electric-fountain-beverly-gardens

Oldest Existing Newspaper: latimes.com/la-mediagroup-times-history-htmlstory.html; Pitt, Leonard; Pitt, Dale, Los Angeles *A-Z, An Encyclopedia of the City and County*, University of California Press, Berkeley and Los Angeles, California, 2000, pgs. 304, 305

Oldest Boat Shop: larsonboat.com/historical; laconservancy.org/locations/al-larson-boat-shop-complex

Oldest Operating Lighthouse: lighthousefriends.com/light.asp?ID=99; sanpedro.com/la-waterfront/angels-gate-lighthouse

Oldest Aquarium: cabrillomarineaquarium.org/_publications/CMA-History-2009.pdf; cabrillomarineaquarium.org/events-news/photo-galleries-details.asp?id=2

Oldest Mission: californiamissionsfoundation.org/mission-san-gabriel; latimes.com/california/story/2020-07-12/san-gabriel-mission-a-symbol-of-faith-history-oppression-bad-damaged-by-fire, San Gabriel Mission, a Symbol of Faith, History and Oppression, is Badly Damaged, *Los Angeles Times*, by Andrew J. Campa, Alex Wigglesworth, Sonali Kohli, July 12, 2020

Oldest Grapevine: latimes.com/food/story/2020-10-09/san-gabriel-mission-wine

Oldest Annual Parade: tournamentofroses.com/about/about-rose-parade/#about

Oldest Independent Bookstore: vromansbookstore.com/vromans-history; laalmanac.com/arts/ar720.php

Oldest Botanical Gardens: huntington.org/about; Hertrich, William, *The Huntington Botanical Gardens*,1949

Oldest Observatory: mtwilson.edu/about-mwo

Oldest Pharmacy: fairoakspharmacy.net/history.html; latimes.com/food/la-fo-re-fair-oaks-pharmacy-20180808-story.html, A 12-Pound Ice Cream Sundae? A Look at the 103-Year-Old Fair Oaks Pharmacy, *Los Angeles Times*, Sara Cagle, Aug.13, 2018

Oldest Outdoor Athletic Stadium: discoverlosangeles.com/visit/rose-bowl-stadium-the-story-of-an-la-icon, Rose Bowl Stadium: The Story of an L.A. Icon, Discover Los Angeles.com, Aug. 21, 2019; visitpasadena.com/directory/rose-bowl-stadium; collegegridirons.com/stadiums/rose-bowl

Oldest Women's Sanitarium: friendsofrockhaven.org/history; laist.com/news/site-of-historic-glendale-mental-health-facility-will-be-turned-into-a-museum, The Site of a Historic Glendale Sanitarium Will Become a Mental Health Museum, Robert Garrova, LAist, July 6, 2021

Oldest Nature Center: sandimascanyonnaturecenter.com/history

Oldest Search and Rescue: nixle.us/D6LJG; Thrilling Tales of Montrose Search and Rescue, Mike Lawler, Fonthill Publishing, 2018

Oldest Children's Bookstore: shoponceuponatime.com/our-story; latimes.com/entertainment-arts/books/story/2020-10-27/once-upon-a-time-childrens-bookstore-covid-19-jimmy-fallon, America's oldest children's bookstore is struggling in the pandemic. But there's hope, Mary McNamara Los Angeles Times, Oct. 27, 2020

Oldest Sheet Music Store: baxternorthup.tumblr.com/history

Oldest Costume Company: westerncostume.com/about-us/history

Oldest Theme Park: themeparkinsider.com/flume/201307/3564/, Theme Park History, a Short History of Universal Studios Hollywood, Robert Niles; thestudiotour.com/ush/chronology.php

Oldest Rectangular, Thin Crust Pizza: baronesfamousitalian.com/about.html; deanjab.com/2014/11/barones-famous-italian-restaurant-valley-glen-california

Oldest Chili House: chilijohnsofca.com/about.php

Oldest Gold Discovery Site: laweekly.com/
the-incredible-story-of-californias-first-
gold-strike-takes-place-just-minutes-from-
downtown-l-a; latimes.com/archives/la-xpm-
1990-03-08-vw-2800-story.html

Oldest Oil Boomtown: mrca.ca.gov/parks/
park-listing/mentryville; visitsantaclarita.
com/things-to-do/historic-points-of-interest/
mentryville; scvhistory.com/mentryville

Oldest Restaurant: laalmanac.com/economy/
ec15h.php; scvhistory.com/scvhistory/
sauguscafe.htm; visitsantaclarita.com/dining/
restaurants/saugus-cafe

Oldest Still-Standing Jailhouse: scvhistory.
com/scvhistory/sd0200.htm; walkingtour.
oldtownnewhall.com/locations/i/15865752/
old-newhall-jail-old-town-newhall

Oldest Dam Disaster: smithsonianmag.com/
history/occasions-i-envy-dead-st-francis-dam-
disaster-180954543/, On Occasions Like This,
I Envy the Dead: The St. Francis Dam Disaster,
Matt Blitz, Smithsonian Magazine, March 12,
2015; damfailures.org/case-study/st-francis-
dam-california-1928; santaclaritaguide.com/
StFrancisDamTours.html

Oldest Hotel: thelog.com/catalina-connection/
catalina-islands-oldest-hotel-glenmore-plaza-
hotel-holds-captivating-history

Oldest Fishing Club: lovecatalina.com/island-
info/historic-landmarks/the-tuna-club;
islapedia.com/index.php?title=Tuna_Club,_
Avalon,_Santa_Catalina_Island

Oldest Family-Owned Boat Company:
islapedia.com/index.php?title=Catalina_
Speed_Boat_Company; latimes.com/travel/
la-xpm-2013-may-05-la-tr-avalon-20130505-
story.html, Santa Catalina's famous past
is found in its charming present, Rose
McClure, *Los Angeles Time*s, May 5, 2013;
catalinaexpress.com/about-us.html

Oldest Circular Ballroom: visitcatalinaisland.
com/about-the-island/history/catalina-casino;
laconservancy.org/locations/catalina-casino

INDEX